ALL IT TAKES IS GUTS

A Minority View

ALL IT TAKES IS GUTS

A Minority View

WALTER E. WILLIAMS

REGNERY BOOKS
Washington, D.C.

Library of Congress Cataloging-in-Publication Data

Williams, Walter E. (Walter Edward), 1936–
    All it takes is guts : a minority view / Walter E. Williams.
        p.   cm.
    ISBN 0-89526-569-9 : $16.95
    1. Laissez-faire.   2. United States—Economic policy.
    3. Minorities—Employment—United States. 4. Women—Employ-
ment—United States.   I. Title.
    HB95.W538 1987
    338.973—dc19   87-18161
                                                                CIP

Published in the United States by
Regnery Gateway
1130 17th Street, NW
Washington, DC 20036

Distributed to the trade by
Kampmann & Company, Inc.
9 E 40th Street
New York, NY 10016
10 9 8 7 6 5 4 3 2 1

CONTENTS

ACKNOWLEDGMENTS

S O MANY of my ideas break with conventional wisdom that the average person might reasonably ask why I think the way I do. This brief acknowledgment might help answer the question.

An unpayable debt of gratitude goes to my mother, who taught me to be independent, suspicious of the status quo, and ambitious. She assumed the challenging job of raising two children—alone, after her husband abandoned her—through the depression years, fighting the influences of the slums.

It must have been an act of Providence for me to encounter teachers like: Dr. Martin Rosenberg at Benjamin Franklin High School (1950-54), Professor Arthur Kirsch at California State University Los Angeles, where I earned a Bachelor of Arts degree, and professors Armen Alchian, Clayburn LaForce, Axel Leijonhufvud, and others at UCLA, where I earned my doctorate in economics. All these teachers had one thing in common: They recognized my academic deficiencies, challenged me, and gave me *real* help. They gave their personal time and held me accountable to high standards. In today's era of "enlightened" racial relationships, all too often misguided teachers hold many black students accountable to low standards in the name of "taking into account past discrimination."

Acknowledgment must also go to numerous friends, associates, and colleagues who offered me valuable criticism. I have also benefited from the many letters, both pro and con, from readers of my column.

A word of thanks and appreciation goes to the Heritage Features Syndicate of the Heritage Foundation, which syndicates my column, and to its editor, Mr. Andrew Seamans, for his graciously allowing me to reprint my columns here.

I thank my secretary/assistant Mrs. Marion Friedlander for her help in running down information, catching my mistakes in grammar, and cheerfully typing and retyping innumerable drafts.

Finally, a very special debt of gratitude goes to my wife, Connie, whom I married 27 years ago and who has given me the intestinal fortitude to persevere over some tough years, and who, at just the right time, awarded me with my daughter, Devon, whom I cherish.

PREFACE

I BELIEVE the unprecedented freedom and wealth Americans enjoy is at once a curiosity and a predictable outcome. It is a curiosity because man's most frequent fate is to be controlled arbitrarily, by others. In centuries past, Kings, Lords, and petty underlings simply rode into villages and confiscated property for their coffers and commandeered men for their armies. The common man was subject to governmental whims and mandates without recourse. Equality before the law was an alien concept. Freedom of religion, speech, and the press were all but unknown. Today, for most people, well-organized and far more powerful governments have replaced Kings and Lords, but arbitrary control and oppression continues.

The United States is an exception to the pattern of human abuse. Americans are the freest people in the history of mankind. That is the curiosity. Why us? Why were our Founding Fathers suspicious of the Westminster system of government where the Parliament's wisdom is beyond judicial question. When the Framers of the Constitution finished their task, why were they sympathetic to Thomas Jefferson's and George Mason's insistence on the addition of a Bill of Rights to hamstring government with a list of particulars where "Congress shall make no law. . . ." No doubt these men were familiar with the writings of philosophers like Locke, Hume, Mill, and Adam Smith, and understood that human abuse was a natural result of unbridled government power. This knowledge existed elsewhere, but it was the Framers who made the best use of it.

The United States is not only the freest nation in the world, it is also the wealthiest. Some people think we are rich because of our bountiful natural resources. But if a rich endowment of natural resources can explain wealth, then why are some of the world's poorest people citizens of continents richest in natural resources, such as Africa and South America. By contrast, Japan, Hong Kong, Switzerland, and England are poor in natural resources, but their citizens enjoy living standards among the highest in the world.

It is frequently asserted that the "Third World" is poor because of colonial domination that enriched the mother country at the expense of the colony. But some of the richest nations in the world were colonies—the United States, Canada, and Australia—and Hong Kong remains a colony. By contrast, some of the world's poorest countries were never colonies—such as Ethiopia and Liberia. If colonial "exploitation" is a satisfactory explanation for Third World poverty, we need a theory to explain the exceptions.

Poverty is an uninteresting subject. Poverty has been, and continues to be, man's standard fate throughout his entire history. The reason is simple. People are poor because they cannot produce much that is valued by others. The intriguing question is why a *tiny* percentage of the world's population, for only a *tiny* part of man's history, has been spared man's usual fate. If we could answer that question, America's wealth could be readily duplicated throughout the world.

While nobody has the complete answer, there are some clues, hunches, and bits of circumstantial evidence. Freedom is the connection. Where we find riches, we tend to find freer people. An examination of Amnesty International's listings of human rights abuses shows a definite pattern where those nations with the least respect for human rights are also the poorest. By contrast, those with the greatest respect for human rights tend to be the richest.

Such a finding is consistent with philosopher-economist Adam Smith's propositions in his famous book, *An Inquiry into the Nature and Causes of the Wealth of Nations.* Current rhetoric sees Smith's advocacy of *laissez-faire* as an apology for greedy businessmen at the expense of the common man. That is a grievously wrong assessment of Adam Smith's message. In fact, I challenge any reader to find a single passage in *The Wealth of Nations* that can be reasonably interpreted as pro-business.

Smith, as a moral philosopher, was laying out a moral way for men to interact with one another. Smith argues that voluntary association is *the* moral way for men to interact, and that it produces riches as an *unintended* result. *The Wealth of Nations,* published in 1776, had a profound influence on the Framers of the Constitution. Adam Smith saw government as a *referee,* not a player, in the game of life. For Smith, the legitimate role of government was: national defense, adjudication of disputes, and provision of some public goods. In 1801, Thomas Jefferson echoed these sentiments in his first inaugural address: "A wise and frugal government, which shall restrain men from injuring one another, which shall leave them otherwise free to regulate their own pursuits of industry and improvement, and shall not take from the mouth of labor the bread it has earned. This is the sum of good government. . . ."

The American values of limited government and personal freedom have been under assault for nearly a century. Out of a misguided sense of concern for our fellow man we have permitted, and even called for, government to restrain many important freedoms. The tragedy is that most Americans do not realize or appreciate what is happening—they do not understand that our freedom is being reduced by small bits at a time. The late Leonard Read of the Foundation for Economic Education said that Americans will never lose their freedom all at once. Such an attempt would encounter massive resistance. To take American freedom, Read continued, was like cooking a frog. Read warned you cannot cook a frog by tossing him into a pot of boiling water. The frog's reflexes are so quick that as soon as his feet touched the water, he would leap out and escape. The way to cook a frog is to put him in a pot of cold water and turn up the heat a little at a time. By the time the frog realized he was being cooked, it would be too late.

That scenario explains what has been happening in America. We have not been losing freedom in big, noticeable chunks; we have been losing it little by little. Erosion of our personal freedoms, in the name of "higher" ideals, is the theme of this selected collection of my nationally syndicated columns, which were published in roughly 80 newspapers in the United States from 1982 to 1987. I have no shame in admitting my uncompromising bias for the sanctity of personal freedom and freely admit that as economist *qua* columnist I try to sell Americans on the moral superiority of individual freedom.

ALL IT TAKES IS GUTS

A Minority View

Chapter I

RACE AND SEX

T HE FACT of race and sex discrimination in the United States does not make us unique. There is no place on the globe free of race and sex discrimination of one form or another. The truly unique feature of the United States is our effort to eliminate discrimination. Our greatest achievement is that the typical American of today finds race and sex discrimination repulsive.

Civil rights organizations and feminist organizations are quick to assert that discrimination explains income, and other, differences. But can race discrimination alone explain the fact that black median income is only 59 percent that of whites? Can sex discrimination alone explain why female median income is only 61 percent that of males?

An improper diagnosis can lead to an inappropriate policy prescription. If we diagnose the high rate of black teenage unemployment (45 percent) as the result of employer racism, when, in fact, poor education is a more significant factor, then any anti-discrimination policy will produce disappointing results.

If high crime rates, high illegitimacy, the breakdown of the black family, and the destruction of black neighborhoods are interpreted as a result of racism, we will suffer the same disappointment. Whether racial discrimination exists or not is not the critical issue; more important is

3

how *much* of what we see is caused by racial discrimination and how much is caused by other factors.

The same is true of sex discrimination. The fact that the median income of women is roughly 61 percent that of males is frequently cited as evidence of discrimination. But unmarried men earn only 65 percent the earnings of married men, and never-been-married women, who remain in the labor force from age 18 to 37, earn slightly more than never-been-married men of the same description. Never-been-married female college professors with the same qualifications as their male counterparts earn slightly more than their never-been-married male counterparts.

These male/female differences are far too complicated to be explained by the familiar refrain: discrimination. Many differences in income reflect personal choices about marriage, job location, study choices, life styles, etc.

In the columns that follow, I challenge the conventional thinking on race and sex discrimination.

Quotas Are Unconstitutional

ONE ASPECT of the fairness issue the Reagan administration catches hell on is its civil rights record. Critics rightfully point out that President Reagan, the Justice Department, and his new Civil Rights Commission appointees are against race and sex quotas. This writer shares the administration's position, but in view of the 1984 elections it appears that the administration is beginning to cave in to antagonistic pressures.

Some Americans think quotas are justified in light of gross past injustices suffered by blacks and women; they argue for a special advantage here and there for these groups. But the sad, immutable fact of life is you can't give one person or group a special advantage without simultaneously subjecting another to a special *disadvantage*. This raises the question of why should someone else suffer a disadvantage or a punishment.

Let's take, for example, the white kid who's denied admission to a particular college in order to meet quota requirements for a black kid. How is that white youth accountable for slavery and past oppression of blacks? Or a more personal example: If I'm denied a job because a company must meet female quotas, I feel mistreated. I never did anything to oppress women. I didn't write sexually discriminatory laws. Why should I be punished?

These problems may soon have their day in court under constitutional

5

prohibitions against legislatures enacting a bill of attainder (U.S. Constitution, Article 1, Section 9, Paragraph 3). (A bill of attainder is a legislative determination of guilt and imposition of punishment upon a specified group or specified individuals without the safeguards of a judicial trial.) Technically, according to David Butler writing in the *Drake Law Review* (1983), an act is a bill of attainder when the punishment is death. Otherwise, and more appropriate to quota discussion, they are bills of pains and penalties which also fall into the scope of constitutional prohibition.

To show that quotas fall into the scope of a bill of attainder, "punishment of some specified group," we need merely cite official statements. For example, according to Joseph Califano, President Jimmy Carter told his cabinet, "Get rid of all those who are incompetent, except minorities and women." And Thurgood Marshall, our esteemed Supreme Court associate justice once said, "You guys have been practicing discrimination for years. Now it is our turn." The Equal Employment Opportunity Commission (EEOC) records, while Eleanor Norton was chairing it, contain numerous statements of policy which appear to be constitutionally prohibited.

Ironically, a constitutional test of quotas as a bill of attainder, and subsequent prohibition, would help the Democrats more than it would Republicans. Carter committed the Democrats to racial quotas. Some political observers, like Ben Wattenberg, chairman of the Coalition for a Democratic Majority, argue that Carter's commitment to racial quotas cost him a considerable portion of the blue-collar vote and subsequently contributed a good deal to his losing the 1980 presidential election to Reagan. But the Democrats are on the horns of a dilemma. If they back away from official support of quotas they'll probably gain some white votes, but at the risk of offending blacks and the feminist groups. They could avoid this painful choice if the courts would rule that quotas are a constitutionally prohibited bill of attainder.

So what's my guess? If the Supreme Court, as presently constituted, is forced to rule on racial quotas as a bill of attainder it will "find" them constitutional. The Democrats will publicly soft-pedal racial quotas in '84, telling blacks something different behind closed doors, and follow the Reagan direction on quotas should they capture the White House. But I could be wrong on both counts, so don't bet the rent money.

August 1983

Stupid Theft

"WILLIAMS SPEAKS for the Oppressors," blared an article in the *Cleveland Plain Dealer's* October 12 edition. It carried the byline of *Plain Dealer* reporter George E. Jordan, who boasts that the NAACP and Urban League are responsible for his career in journalism. That shouldn't be surprising; it couldn't have been his journalistic skills and integrity that won him his job.

Jordan's article—a personal attack on this writer—came in the wake of a speech I gave in Cleveland on September 27 for the Ashbrook Memorial Center for Public Affairs, sponsored by Ashland College. The speech, entitled, "Government Intervention and Individual Freedom," was on the legitimate functions of government.

Jordan's attack begins, "At times I wish the Lord would deliver me back to the days of Stepin Fetchit, Aunt Jemima and Uncle Tom. The old-style black illiterate 'handkerchief heads' were an embarrassment, but they were harmless in comparison to 'educated' blacks like economist Walter E. Williams, a darling of the far Right." Jordan goes on, ". . . Williams is a butter-tongued apologist for the new oppressors of the most helpless black Americans." Continuing, he writes, "I could never really get angry at the old Stepin Fetchits and Aunt Jemimas for they were uneducated and simply practicing the art of survival. But I have only contempt for people like Williams. . . ."

Herein lay the gist of Jordan's report; nothing was said of my speech.

But as I read the article I recalled that my colleague, Dr. Thomas Sowell, another black economist, came under similar scurrilous attack by columnist Carl Rowan in the September 29, 1981, *Washington Post*. And no wonder Jordan's assault reminded me of what Rowan said of Sowell. Rowan started off, "These are times when I want to ask the Lord to deliver us back to the days of Stepin Fetchit, Aunt Jemima and Uncle Tom. The old-style black, illiterate, obsequious 'handkerchief heads' were an embarrassment, but they were harmless compared with the 'educated' blacks who are now the darlings of the far Right." Hmmm, sound familiar? Rowan continued to berate Sowell, "I could never really get angry at the old Stepin Fetchits and Aunt Jemimas for they were poorly educated, and just practicing the art of survival. But I have only contempt for today's butter-tongued apologists who are the new oppressors of America's down-and-out people."

Need we go further. Clearly, *Plain Dealer* reporter Jordan plagiarized the Rowan article. If you're unfamiliar with polite academic language, Jordan *copied* Rowan's article, modified it a little to accommodate the attack on me, and passed it off to his employer and the readers of the *Plain Dealer* as his own. Some people describe what Jordan did as theft.

Jordan's plagiarism of a *nationally* syndicated article can best be described as stupid, and we shouldn't expect newspapers to fire reporters merely for stupidity, to do so might decimate the ranks of reporters. But the *Plain Dealer* should fire Jordan. No newspaper can afford blatant, intentional journalistic theft and dishonesty.

We live in a world of racial stereotypes whether we like it or not. Black people cannot afford the likes of Jordan, whose actions parallel those of Janet Cooke, late of *The Washington Post*, who won a Pulitzer Prize that she subsequently had to turn down when her story turned out to be complete fabrication. These people reinforce racist charges of black incompetence. Young blacks fighting to prove themselves can thank people like Jordan and Cooke when managing editors do double and triple takes on their work.

By the way, what was it in my speech that set off Jordan's attack? Essentially I said it was illegitimate use of government power to take the property of one citizen and give it to another, or to give one citizen a privilege which is denied another. Individual liberty has *always* had a way of making some people mad. But I didn't think it would make anyone resort to plagiarism just to vent his anger.

December 1983

Take the Word Segregation

IT WAS Bentham who said, "Error is never so difficult to be destroyed as when it has roots in language." Words can, and often do, have different meanings. Hence arises the difficulty in communication.

Nowhere is there as much confusion in word usage as in matters having to do with race. Take the word segregation. Ask the average American whether the water fountains at the nation's airports are racially segregated. The consensus would be that the water fountains are not segregated. The test people would use to make such a determination is to observe whether a black in the airport could use the fountain without interference.

Now ask the average American whether public schools in the United States are racially segregated. No consensus could be achieved. Some Americans would say "no." Many would say "yes." Such a disagreement on an easy-to-observe phenomenon results from ambiguous use of the word segregation. The word's meaning shifts as we go from water fountains to public schools.

In America today, it would be impossible to find a public school with a whites-only policy. Today, if a black lives on the same street as a white, both can go to the same neighborhood public school.

When people say schools are segregated, they must not mean that

9

blacks and whites living in a particular school zone are prohibited from attendance. They mean that the school does not have what they deem the "right" racial mix. Court-ordered busing is not directed toward desegregating schools; it is directed at producing what a power considers the right racial mix of students.

The problem with sloppy use of terminology is that it leads to sloppy public policy. If we judge that because a school does not have "enough" blacks it is guilty of segregation, we assign guilt and responsibilities to innocent people. A school may not have black students for many reasons that have nothing to do with the school's racial policies, just as in the case of an airport where no blacks use its water fountain. Neither observation necessarily implies racial segregation. What about ice hockey games? At any given game of the Philadelphia Flyers, there are few if any blacks in attendance. In light of the fact that Philadelphia's population is forty percent black, does such an observation suggest that the Flyers maintain a racial segregation policy?

There are many explanations for the racial makeup of a public school that have nothing to do with racial segregation, just as the racial distribution of water fountain users at airports or the racial distribution of ice hockey game attendees may be explained by factors that have nothing to do with racial segregation. It would be a mess if we applied a numbers-based policy to all areas in which the numbers came out "wrong." There is probably no better way to divide people and stir racial animosity than to accuse guiltless people of racism.

Take care with the word segregation.

Spring 1984

How to Fool Some of the
People Most of the Time

CIVILIZED DISCOURSE requires a consensus on what words, symbols, and expressions mean. In mathematics, definitions are nearly perfect. There is, for example, worldwide consensus on the definition of *pi* to the fourth decimal place: 3.1415. Try to reach a similar consensus, just among your friends, on a basic economic question: What are the basic human needs?

Pi has objective, analytical, and operational meaning, but "human needs" is devoid of such scientific features.

People say we "need" water, and in the United States the average per capita daily use of water is 200 gallons. But when we say we need water, does it mean we cannot do with less? Under combat, men have done with less than a quart of water daily and survived.

When we say people need water, food, and shelter, there is no common agreement on what constitutes the exact amount needed. This can become a problem when we act as if such an expression has operational meaning. In reality, it means whatever *anybody* wants it to mean.

Many widely used expressions are rich in emotive content but poor in analytical content. During a crisis, political figures often say "One should not profit from the misfortunes of others." Thank God that statement is not interpreted literally, made law, and strictly enforced.

Consider: You've gone skiing. You had the *misfortune* to break your leg. You go to a physician; he sets it. He has profited from your misfortune. Or your car breaks down; a tow truck driver gets it running. He has profited from your misfortune. There are thousands of ways in which people benefit from the misfortunes of others. Furthermore, the greater the misfortune the greater the benefit.

When people preach against profiting from the misfortune of others, they don't really mean a prohibition of such activities. They probably mean people should not be *exploited*. But what does exploitation mean? There you are, with a broken-down car in the middle of the night. The tow truck driver says he can get you started, but his price is $200. You have several alternatives, among them: seek offers from other emergency repairmen, call a friend, or abandon your car and walk. If you instead *voluntarily* fork over $200, all any other observer can conclude is that you chose what *you* considered your best alternative.

A word like exploitation doesn't seem a good characterization of one's *best* alternative. Would you have been better off had the tow truck not come along? No, one is always better off with a greater number of alternatives from which to choose. Would you have been better off if he charged a lower price? The answer is, yes. And therein lies the most reasonable interpretation of what people may mean by exploitation: a disagreement with price. In other words, had the tow truck driver performed the identical service for $25, we would not rush to call his act exploitation. However, if exploitation is taken to mean we'd like a lower price, then the word exploitation is rendered meaningless because people always prefer lower prices to higher prices. For a word like exploitation to have a chance at operational meaning, it should be left to characterize involuntary exchanges like rape, robbery, fraud, and murder.

Equal employment opportunity is a pleasing expression with great emotive content but no analytical or operational worth. When you hire a plumber to install a faucet, do you give every available plumber an equal employment opportunity? How does one construct a test to determine if you have or not? What if you, as many people do, use the "ole boy" or word-of-mouth system to hire the "right" plumber. Should you be dragged into court under fair employment laws?

Equal employment opportunity might mean that, in dealing with the public, one must use acceptable procedures that prohibit employment discrimination based on sex, age, race, and handicap status. But how can we tell that employment was not based on these outlawed criteria?

Should numbers be the test? Then what about the fact that black males make up well over 70 percent of National Basketball Association players while they constitute less than one percent of professional ice hockey players? Does this finding mean there is or is not equal employment opportunity by race and sex in these two jobs? If not, would you make it equal?

Appended to the issue of equal employment opportunity is a "fairness" issue that is never considered. If fairness requires employers to practice equal employment opportunity, why doesn't it also require *employees* to practice the same. In other words, should economics professor Paul Samuelson give every college an equal opportunity to hire him or should he be permitted to discriminate among employers?

This discussion will not persuade people to purge their vocabularies of ambiguous, nonoperational terminology. Politically astute people often find expressions of great emotional content valuable in the pursuit of personal goals. But questions need to be asked about words that people think are clear and understandable. And when a person uses ambiguous words to attain personal goals by fooling and confusing others, perhaps he should try not to also fool himself.

Fall 1984

Reprinted from the fall, 1984 issue of *The Journalist* by permission of the Foundation for American Communications (FACS).

Political Swaps and Other Bad Deals

For over a decade, this writer has tried to illustrate the devastating effects of the minimum wage law on teenage employment, particularly that of black teenagers. More than 90 percent of what is written by economists about the subject concludes that the minimum wage law reduces employment opportunities for the least-skilled segments of the labor force. The economists only differ on *how much* unemployment is caused by it. The existence of the minimum wage law explains why black teenage unemployment was roughly 10 percent in 1948 (equal to or slightly less than white teenage unemployment) and is now over 50 percent (more than double that of white teens).

You're probably puzzled by the silence of black leaders about the devastating effects of minimum wage laws. That's where the political swaps and bad deals come in. Any black politician coming out against the minimum wage law would lose union political support even though it would benefit a very large part of his constituency. Such a loss means no union campaign contributions. And what's the benefit of coming out against minimum wage laws? More teenagers would be employed. The political problem is teenagers don't vote, but union members and other beneficiaries of the minimum wage law do.

None of this implies that black politicians are fools. They get something back from the unions. The unions lend political support for funny jobs, like CETA jobs. The black politician comes back to his district beating his breast claiming congressional success: "I got you 200 CETA jobs." Of course his vote in support of the minimum wage law might have resulted in the loss of several thousand jobs in the same district.

Most black congressmen vote in support of higher and higher agricultural price supports. They go to their district to cry about hunger in America. Then return to Washington to vote to slaughter milk cows, restrict acreage allotments, and limit the importation of foreign farm products. You don't need a degree in economics to guess all these laws *raise* the price of food.

But again, these black congressmen are not fools; they don't walk away from the deal empty-handed. The farm lobby and those congressmen from farm states say, "Vote with me to raise the price of food, and I'll vote with you to get food stamps for your people." The economics of such a swap are asinine. A full 70 percent of black people receive no food stamps and wouldn't recognize them if you put them on a dish. Thus the possibility: black people may have their food prices raised by $15 billion as a result of farm price supports and as a group receive $4 billion worth of food stamps.

Take heart in all of this. It means there's equal opportunity at last in America: Black politicians rip off their people just as white politicians rip off theirs. I look forward to the evening news broadcast when the reporter asks the "caring" congressman or senator why, if he cares about "hunger," he votes for increases in the price of milk. Or if it was his week to care about the jobless, why did he vote in support of the minimum wage law and literally scores of other laws which create unemployment.

For most Americans political swaps are bad deals.

March 1984

Women and Blacks

D R. THOMAS Sowell, Senior Fellow at the Hoover Institution in Stanford, California, has written another path-breaking book, *Civil Rights: Rhetoric or Reality* (Morrow & Company, 1984, $11.95). Sowell focuses on the "visions" of civil rights: quotas, busing, and other promises for a better world. For an election year steeped in demagoguery, his best chapter is "The Special Case of Women."

The most familiar explanation for occupational and income differences between men and women is that employers discriminate against women. Sowell examines the charge that sex discrimination causes the median income of women to be three-fifths that of men; it's a *non sequitur* that women are paid less for doing the same work.

In reality, the average woman works substantially fewer hours than the average man because a very high proportion of women work part-time. And they average fewer continuous years of employment on a given job. Sowell says a considerable part of the economic differences between men and women are related to marriage. Women who've never been married earn 91 percent of the income of men who've never been married. The remaining 9 percent difference can't be chalked up to discrimination because women typically are not educated in highly paid fields like mathematics, science, and engineering. Nor are they attracted to physically taxing but well-paid fields like construction, lumberjacking, mining, and the like.

In 1971, women who were never married and worked continuously since high school earned slightly more than men of the same description.

Marriage and parenthood have profound economic effects. Marriage *increases* labor market activity of men and *decreases* that of women. The greater the number of children, the greater the number of hours men work and the higher their earnings; it is the opposite with women.

Marriage interrupts the labor-force participation of women. In some fields, just a few years of absence renders certain skills obsolete. For example, in physics a person loses half the value of his knowledge after a six-year layoff. A tax attorney who has missed six years of keeping up with tax legislation and its judicial interpretation cannot be as effective to a client as one who has continuous labor-market experience. But a good librarian, editor, secretary, or teacher is likely to be as good after a six-year layoff as before. Noticeably, women gravitate toward fields with a low obsolescence rate because most women get married.

We all should read Sowell's *Civil Rights* to separate the sense from the nonsense about women. Sowell makes no denial of the existence of sex discrimination. His research merely proves sexism cannot explain all, or even most, of the differences between the sexes.

August 1984

Women Will Lose
If Feminists Win

THE FEMALE struggle against sex discrimination has taken a new and insidious turn in recent years. This observation doesn't apply to women in general but to those feminist organizations, such as the National Organization for Women (NOW), which *claim* to represent women.

Let me state at the outset: I find sexual inequality before the law offensive. In fact, I find *any* law which treats one person differently than another offensive. In this respect, women have a legitimate gripe; in the past we've had many laws which discriminated against women. There *were* so-called "protective" laws, which banned women from many jobs such as tending bar and mining. Other laws discriminated by making it illegal for women to lift weights in excess of 35 pounds, or to work during night hours or on weekends. These and other laws were sought by labor unions to increase the cost of hiring women so men would have less competition and hence higher wages. Labor unions have used (and still use) similar strategy to keep blacks, children, and immigrants out of jobs.

Another justifiable grievance of women at the hands of the state was the fact they could not vote until the ratification in 1920 of the 19th Amendment to the U.S. Constitution. The fact that women were prohibited from voting was *not,* in my opinion, a flaw in the Constitution, but rather a defect in court interpretations. Read the Constitution; you'll see *no* reference to sex. The terminology of the Constitution and the Bill of

Rights, as well as our Declaration of Independence, is gender-neutral; it uses words like: persons, people, citizen. That means, of course, the Equal Rights Amendment is at best superfluous.

But radical feminist organizations are not demanding equality before the law; they seek to use the law to subvert individual freedom and decision-making. This is most apparent in their push for so-called equal pay for *comparable worth* and "unisex" insurance laws.

Radical feminists argue that since the median income of women still is 59 percent that of men, equal pay for *equal work* and anti-sex discrimination laws have failed. They allege women's work is paid a lower wage; therefore, they say typists and truck drivers may be of "comparable worth" to the employer and should receive the same pay. NOW wants to repeal the laws of supply-and-demand and replace them with the "just" wage, a discredited, nonsensical, medieval notion of compensation.

The fact that women, on average, live longer than men requires that pension programs—for the same premium—give women smaller pension checks. If they didn't, the pension plan would be actuarily unsound. Feminists view this policy as yet another form of sex discrimination and want laws requiring equal pension checks.

Comparable worth laws will do for women what minimum wage laws have done to blacks and teenagers. It will price all but the most skilled women out of the market. Companies will respond to higher wage costs, uncompensated by greater productivity, with mechanization and by exporting jobs to cheap-labor foreign sources. Only elite women will benefit, which might explain why feminists haven't been successful in enlisting poor women to their movement.

Unisex insurance laws will cause women to pay higher auto insurance. Based on accident claim experience, insurance companies charge men higher rates than women. Unisex laws would require women to pay as much as men. But the scenario wouldn't end there because per $1,000 of life insurance a person age 50 pays a higher premium than a person age 20. If there can be no sex differences in insurance, can there be age discrimination? We'd have a "uni-age" law. It would be like quotas. Once blacks got them, everybody else wanted them.

The bottom line is that radical feminists want to use government to alter or cancel the independent decisions of millions of people. These shortsighted women are like any other group of totalitarians.

September 1984

19

Racism, Sexism, and Nonsense!

THESE ARE the times that try men's souls. My heart really goes out to white people and men. I first really noticed their dilemma when I interviewed for a job at a fairly prestigious university. First, I was taken to meet the university's "affirmative action" lady, then to the chairman of the Afro-American Studies Department, and, finally, to a group of black students. On the way to a luncheon to meet the economics faculty chairman I asked whether this was the department's standard hiring procedure. He said no, explaining he thought I'd feel more comfortable knowing there was a black community on campus. I told him, to the contrary, I was more uncomfortable wondering whether there was an economic community on campus.

You can just see it. This poor fellow was probably told the reason he couldn't recruit blacks was due to his insensitivity. Lo and behold, he tries to be sensitive and here comes economist Williams.

A variation of this dilemma is Fritz Mondale's plight. In a recent speech to Temple University students, the Reverend Louis Farrakhan declared Mondale a racist. Mondale didn't lynch anybody or use a racial slur; he had a few blacks working on his campaign. Sniffing the political winds, Mondale was no longer calling for the resurrection of the Great

Society, the busing of students, or for hiring quotas. Today that makes you a racist.

To be a racist today, you don't have to be some bigwig like Bull Connors or George Wallace. You can be a "little" man. In the recent District of Columbia primary, Carol Schwartz, a white Republican, defeated the Reverend Jerry Moore, a black Democrat. D.C. Mayor Marion Barry and Delegate Walter Fauntroy, according to *The Washington Post,* made the unproven charge that Moore's defeat was due to racism.

Carrying this kind of reasoning to its conclusion suggests that by November 5 we will be a nation of racists. The logic is simple and indisputable. Clearly, whoever votes for a racist is himself a racist. Farrakhan has declared Mondale a racist; Reagan has been charged with this defect for well over ten years. Therefore, whoever votes for Mondale or Reagan is a racist.

This is a serious charge, and it's a good idea to have some lesser charges to distinguish the average Joe from experts like the Ku Klux Klan and the Nazis. There should be categories like: involuntary racism, no-fault racism, and incidental racism.

Involuntary racism could apply to people who erroneously vote for so-called racists. Then there are those who live in areas like, say, Idaho, who have few if any blacks at their parties. These would be racists through no fault of their own. And incidental racism covers the case where a black is invited to a dance only to be danced to death by having to dance with every girl.

You can be a sexist just as easily. Columnist Art Buchwald, in giving advice about Geraldine Ferraro, said if you stand up when Ferraro enters a room, or assist her getting out of a car, you are guilty of treating her differently than you treat a man. That is sexism.

You might organize a company football team and omit female employees. That's sexism. But suppose you have a 50-50 mixed team, and you tell your wife you will be home late because you're practicing plays with a woman; that's not sexism, it's suicide.

Since it's so easy to be a sexist, we need the same categories there too, like: involuntary sexism, incidental sexism, and sexism through no fault of your own. But what we *really need* is common sense—and the guts to put an end to all this nonsense.

October 1984

An Offbeat Look
at Economics

Lᴇᴛ's ᴛᴀᴋᴇ a look at economics in general. Sound complicated? Or boring? Some people think economics is only about taxes, the stock market, deficits, regulation, and such. Well, it's not. Economics is about everyday things too—like love, litter, and children. Whenever or wherever there is exchange, knowledge of economic theory can add to its understanding.

Advice columnist Ann Landers caused quite a stir with her recent survey concluding that three-quarters of the nation's married women would rather be cuddled than "do the act." Your first impression might be that something awful has happened to men. Economic theory suggests there has always been a falloff in romance after marriage. Women say, "He wasn't like that when we were dating." They're right. Of course he used to open the car door, and shave everyday, on top of being affectionate; he was competing with other men.

But marriage ends competition, creating a monopoly. And we all know that despite some benefits, there are some inefficiencies in having a monopoly. Wives are not immune to the pitfalls of a monopoly. They, like men, put on some excess weight, or become somewhat less attentive to their personal appearance.

A monopoly also can produce other effects in the family. We've all heard that the "only" child tends to be spoiled. We shouldn't be surprised. He has a monopoly on parental affection. As with any monopolist, he can get away with charging a higher "price" for his exclusivity. He can wheedle more out of his parents. After all, he doesn't have sisters and brothers competing and sharing with him.

Competition plays a great role in setting the terms of all exchanges. Suppose you saw a fat, ugly, old, cigar-smoking man married to a beautiful young woman, what conclusion would you draw regarding his income? Right, you'd probably guess it was pretty high. Economists say the man is offering a *compensating* difference. The guy says, "I don't have other guys' looks, but I got money."

Ladies can take advantage of offers to pay compensating differences. If you're tired of dining at Wendy's and want to dine at a fine French restaurant, find an old man with money. Men can take advantage, too. In fact, they've even written songs about it. One Latin favorite has a line that goes, "If you want to be happy for the rest of your life, just make an ugly woman your wife."

Now some people will argue: "Williams, that's using people!" Of course, and "use" is the basis of any relationship. My wife has, on occasion, said, "You're using me." My response, "Honey, if I had no use for you, we wouldn't be married. And I presume you feel the same way." In fact, marriage is a contractual arrangement where people use one another in mutually agreeable and advantageous ways. And the plight of people who can't get a date or get married is that they can't find somebody to use them. People might call them love-starved; an economist might call them love-unemployed.

Speaking of my wife, she worries about my getting home safely what with all the fools on the road. In my opinion she worries because she has me underinsured. With more insurance she might root for the trucks. (Just fooling, dear.)

Economics not only applies to love, it applies to litter as well. How many times do we read or hear the phrase: "Don't litter!"? The inference is that the optimal amount of littering is always zero. Thank God people don't really behave that way. Imagine World War II's Normandy invasion with thousands of troops firing automatic weapons, leaving spent shells all over the place. The captain shouts to his men, "Advance!" The men reply, "Wait, sir, we have to pick up the litter."

Or how would you like to be with a non-littering audience at a baseball game with people constantly getting up saying, "Pardon me, could you let me get through to go to the trash can." As it stands, people begrudge you going in front of them to go to the bathroom. The bottom line is that: too little littering is inefficient and so is too much. The question is how much is the right amount?

Isn't economics fun?

April 1985

New Nonsense from NOW

Dᴇsᴄʀɪʙɪɴɢ ᴛʜᴇ National Organization for Women's (NOW's) call for equal pay for comparable worth, U.S. Civil Rights Commission Chairman Clarence Pendleton called it the looniest idea since "Looney Tunes."

NOW's drive for comparable worth provides normal people with comfort of sorts. Radical feminists can't find enough garden-variety sex discrimination, which has been remedied under existing laws, so they direct their attention to new crusades that strain the boundaries of lucidity.

According to NOW, secretaries are as valuable to a company as truck drivers. But since secretaries are predominantly female and truck drivers predominantly male, employers pay secretaries less. That, according to NOW, is sex discrimination that would be eliminated by a proposed law calling for equal pay for comparable worth. NOW says both jobs should be evaluated through a point system which takes into account skills, training, and effort.

What NOW is advocating is the revival of the discredited medieval idea of the Just Price. Economists long ago discovered the value of anything is *subjective*. There is no way one can objectively measure something inherently arbitrary. It's like asking, "Which is inherently more valuable: an apple or an orange?" It's a subjective question that cannot be made objective by assigning points. You still have an arbitrary item, but now it has meaningless points assigned to it.

Better yet, consider two people working at different jobs. Mary's job is carving complex circuits on computer chips, an occupation requiring high manual dexterity and good eye/muscle coordination and control. Harry's job is carving the Lord's Prayer on a wooden nickel. It requires skills identical to Mary's. A comparable-worth wage commission, evaluating the two jobs, might assign them identical points and hence mandate equal pay. But even the most mindless person could see that the jobs are of different value to society.

Therefore, the value of a job is determined not only by the skills of the worker but also by the value society places on his final product. Were the feminists to have their way in the cited example, we could easily have as many people employed inscribing wooden nickels as making circuits on silicon chips.

Much of the sympathy received by the radical feminists stems from the "59 percent cliché." This says, while women are just as productive as men, they only earn 59 cents for each dollar on average that men earn. The 59 percent cliché requires that we believe male employers, out of stupidity, kindness, or blind allegiance to the brotherhood, are paying men wages 41 percent higher than if they hired an equally productive woman.

If such a cost differential were the case, you can bet some other company would hire the equally productive women and drive the sexist firm out of business. Companies have been driven to the industrial trash heap because they had costs only 2 percent higher than their competitors, much less 41 percent.

If the NOW people would bother to check, they'd find that women who were never married and worked continuously from high school to their mid-thirties earn just as much as men of the same description. Unmarried female academics with the same number of publications, same years of experience, and same quality of education earned slightly *more* than unmarried male academics with the same qualifications. Women, as a group, for good reasons, make choices different from men. The choices affect their careers and pay. The market differences we see reflect those choices. The push for equal pay for comparable worth ignores them.

May 1985

Uncle Sam's Economic
Racism

WILLIAM RASPBERRY, the syndicated columnist, recently wondered why, in the face of rising economic vitality, unemployment among blacks is increasing. "Not only does no one seem to know," Raspberry wrote, "but the government seems uninterested in finding out."

Raspberry has it all wrong. We *do* know why many blacks are immune to economic prosperity, but few people—particularly black politicians and civil rights organizations—are willing to take heed. Furthermore, there may be little political payoff for policies to ameliorate the plight of the most desperately needy blacks.

For more than a decade, economist Thomas Sowell and I have been pointing out how the public education establishment wantonly destroys the career chances of many blacks. We have argued for educational vouchers or tuition tax credits as a way out of the mess. Instead, black leaders called for higher educational budgets, higher teacher pay, and busing. Their response to achievement test scores showing blacks three to five years behind the national norm and to blacks' aptitude test scores 100 points below the norm has been to call the tests racist. The NAACP's and Urban League's response to campaigns for competency testing of teachers and students was the same—"racism."

Another fact of black existence is a crime rate that is just like a law mandating, "There shall be no economic development in black neighborhoods." A tiny percentage of the black community makes life a living nightmare for its law-abiding majority. These thugs make economic activity a costly proposition for white *or* black merchants. Places that were once bustling economic centers in black neighborhoods, such as 125th Street in Harlem, are now wastelands. Black residents who once shopped in neighborhood markets must now trek out to suburban shopping malls. Schools in black neighborhoods have become centers for holdups, murder, and wanton property destruction. Over 50 percent of US homicide victims are blacks murdered by blacks.

All this devastation brought to the attention of black leaders, politicians, and civil rights organizations evokes one response: "Blaming the victim!" Crime is the result of a racist society, they say, never bothering to explain why blacks were more secure and experienced more economic vitality in their communities in *earlier* periods. So for fear of being labeled a racist, white politicians say or do little about crime in black neighborhoods, so long as it's black on black.

The causes of black unemployment are no mystery. Black teenage unemployment is at an unprecedented 47 percent, and over 70 percent in cities like Detroit. Black adult unemployment stands at 16 percent. Immunity to recent economic growth is not a result of any single factor—it is part of a general pattern of carrots and sticks.

First, the carrots. Government programs—unemployment compensation, food stamps, and welfare—make unemployment less painful. We all know that if something is subsidized, be it wheat, cheese, poverty, or unemployment, we can expect more of it. Poor people are like the rest of us. They respond to incentives. Why give up $10,000 a year in nontaxable welfare benefits for a job paying $6,000 or $7,000 a year that's taxable?

Then there are sticks. The minimum wage law acts as an effective barrier to jobs and training prospects for low-skilled youths. Prior to the minimum wage escalation that started in the 1950s, unemployment was lower for teenage blacks than teenage whites. Blacks in *all* age groups were *more* active in the labor market than whites. This was before black politicians did the political bidding of labor unions who sought to restrict employment in order to get higher wages for union members. The *quid pro quo* is that black politicians get political backing from labor unions and black people get the unemployment line.

Moreover, governments at all levels enact more and more regulatory legislation, such as exclusive collective bargaining laws, occupational and business licensing laws, child labor laws, and many forms of wage regulation—all of which further restrict the labor market. And a lot of this was done or maintained with the support of black politicians and civil rights groups.

Unlike my friend Bill Raspberry, I understand why a person who's received a grossly fraudulent education, lived in a neighborhood rife with crime and social disorder, resided in a single-parent household, learned the ways of welfarism, and faces laws that require an employer to pay him more than he's worth (or not hire him at all) is immune to economic prosperity.

But again, what's the political payoff for a politician to do something about it? President Reagan has resubmitted his proposal to permit teenagers to work for less than the minimum wage, thereby creating more employment and greater job-training opportunities. To the Black Caucus, the NAACP, and the Urban League, the proposal is mere reconfirmation that Reagan's a racist. Reagan also calls for deregulation, yet black leaders see this as insensitivity.

Black people do not deserve their political leaders—leaders who support economic dependency. Should Raspberry, or anybody else, be surprised to find many blacks addicted to welfare and immune to economic growth?

June/July 1985

Don't the Media Respect Black 'Leaders'?

"**A**ND THAT'S the way it is," as the major network news winds up its broadcast, America sits down to dinner knowing blacks are against the death penalty, blacks are pro-busing, blacks support racial quotas, and—under the Reagan administration—blacks are going backwards. And the reason Americans are so sure of all this? Why, because the media picked out a black representative and asked, "What do black people think?"

It really makes you wonder. Does the media put House Speaker Tip O'Neill on the airwaves to pontificate about how white people think? No. They don't even ask Reagan how white people think, and he led an unprecedented 49 state electoral sweep in 1984! Were a reporter to ask Reagan, "How do white people think?" he would be reprimanded, if not fired, for asking a foolish, childish question. But somehow, that same intellectual reasoning and respect is not extended to blacks.

It took the general public a while to learn that all black people don't look alike. The task that faces our modern-day media is to get over the myth that all blacks think alike and can have their views represented by a "spokesman"—like Jesse Jackson, Benjamin Hooks, or some baseball player.

Help's on the way. *The Washington Post* recently reported on a survey by Linda Lichter, co-director of the Center for Media and Public Affairs, that polled a random sample of 600 blacks on several questions:

* Should minorities receive preferential treatment to make up for past discrimination? Seventy-seven percent of black leaders said *yes;* the same percentage of the black public said *no*.

* The death penalty for murderers was favored by 55 percent of blacks; only 33 percent of black "leaders" favored capital punishment.

* Sixty-eight percent of black leaders approved of forced school busing for racial balance; 53 percent of the black citizenry disapproved.

Other questions were asked of the 105 leaders of the NAACP, National Urban League, Southern Christian Leadership Conference, Operation PUSH, National Conference of Black Mayors, and Congressional Black Caucus. Their responses routinely differed—significantly—from that of the black public. For the media to listen to the self-serving views of the few, and pass these opinions off as *the* black view, is nothing less than an insult, deserving of some effort to set the record straight.

But that's not the end to racial insults. When Benjamin Hooks, executive director of the NAACP, was informed of the results of the poll he said he "distrusted" the survey. Hooks said that "in these kinds of public opinion polls, the average man on the street, white or black, wants to appear fair. He responds to what the question says. Black leaders are more likely to respond to what the question means." A charitable interpretation of Hooks' statement is that black people don't know what the questions mean and black leaders have to do the thinking. That's a pretty bold supposition with fairly clear racial connotations.

Lest we leave the impression that the media insults *all* black people, let's make it clear they are *somewhat* selective. When Jesse Jackson feeds the reporters a line like, "We're going from the outhouse to the White House," or "From disgrace to amazing grace," or some such inane rhyming preachment there's never a reportorial query, such as "What does that mean?" But let Dr. Thomas Sowell or me say, "Our investigations show the minimum wage has a devastating unemployment effect on black youth," and media people ask all kinds of searching statistical and theoretical questions about our evidence. In fact, they even dig into our personal, financial, and educational backgrounds, the way they dig at the President and other leaders who dispute the views of the black "leadership."

In other words, the media treat us just like white people. It would be nice if they'd extend that same "respect" to black people in general.

October 1985

31

Nonsense and Public Policy

SMOKE DETECTORS save lives. Cigarette smoking increases the chances of lung cancer. Seatbelt use reduces serious injuries and fatalities in highway accidents. Home insulation reduces heating and cooling costs. These are just a few of the thousands of theories that help form the basis of personal behavior and public policy. They have been subjected to ruthless and unyielding examination.

There are other theories, for which we have no evidence of support, that shape public policy and force us to spend billions of dollars. And those who question the validity of these theories risk verbal abuse and public embarrassment.

The theory of civil rights activists is that but for racial discrimination the percentage of blacks in universities, the workplace, and jails would be in proportion to black representation in the population. Furthermore, they theorize that any deviation from proportional representation indicates the presence of—and may be used to measure—discrimination.

There is *no* evidence whatsoever to support the "racial proportional representation" theory. Even when we examine activities where discrimination is impossible we don't find racial proportionality. Fifty percent of Mexican-American wives marry in their teens; only 10 percent of Japanese-American wives marry that young. Far fewer blacks attend ice hockey games than do Irish-Americans. Asian-American Ph.D. economists outnumber black Ph.D. economists three to one. Racial groups differ in child-rearing practices, recreational activities, and their choice of television programs.

Thomas Sowell says, in *Civil Rights,* "Of the five highest totals of home runs in a lifetime, three are by blacks. . . . But of the ten highest slugging averages in a season, seven are by players of German ancestry . . . of the five times that someone has stolen 100 or more bases in a season, all were by black players." In addition, 75 percent of National Basketball Association players are black and so are nearly 50 percent of baseball and 35 percent of football players.

Despite the lack of evidence to support the racial proportionality theory, courts mandate laws as if it were valid. Judges decree that blacks or Hispanics be hired until their numbers on the job are proportional to their numbers in the community.

Then there's the "role model" theory. Sociologists say the absence of good role models is part of the explanation for black educational under-achievement. But Washington has predominately black teachers, a black school superintendent, and a black mayor, yet the District of Columbia's black student academic achievement record leaves much to be desired. On the other hand, Japanese academic achievement is about the highest in the nation, yet Japanese school teachers are few and far apart. So much for the role model theory.

The theory of "comparable worth" says it is possible to measure the value of each job to determine whether female secretarial workers, say, are being underpaid compared to male truck drivers. It is impossible to measure objectively something that is inherently subjective. Asking whether a secretary is as valuable as a truck driver is like asking whether an apple is as valuable as a pear. Even left-of-center economists like Lester Thurow, Paul Samuelson, or James Tobin would say objective measures of value are impossible, but our "learned" judges and practical politicians proceed undaunted.

My theory on judges and politicians who accept invalid theory as gospel is that they are either good but ignorant souls, or that they are intelligent but politically expedient folks, who would use theoretical nonsense as a means to control our private lives.

November 1985

33

Rising Above Principle

THE PRESIDENT has said racial quotas are offensive to the principles of fair play. Such a stance reflects the moral values of most Americans, including blacks. We can't blame quotas on the 1964 Civil Rights Act. By language and intent it expressly prohibited racial quotas. Quotas got their start with President Johnson's Executive Order 11246 and Nixon's Revised Order Number 4, which led to the setting of "goals and timetables" to be enforced by the Office of Federal Contract Compliance.

Our Constitution prohibits unilateral executive action to eliminate destructive taxation and spending; the president needs Congress to accomplish this. Executive orders are another matter. Ronald Reagan can rescind Executive Order 11246 with the stroke of his executive pen. Thus, if quotas persist beyond 1986, the President and his administration are directly responsible.

Much of the controversy surrounding this administration has resulted from its stated opposition to quotas. Attorney General Ed Meese and his assistant, Brad Reynolds, have rightfully argued that quotas are immoral, constitutional violations, and racially divisive. The White House in consultation with the Justice Department and other members of the cabinet, has drafted proposed changes in Executive Order 11246

34

that would eliminate employment quotas. But now, led by Labor Secretary William Brock, the administration is waffling.

The question is why? First, we all know that on principle the Reagan administration is against quotas. But we also know that politicians are experts at learning how to rise above principle and do the "right" thing. The Republicans might have their eyes on the 1986 and 1988 elections. Wishing to attract more blacks and Mexican-Americans, the pols don't want to rock the boat. But surveys show blacks are against preferential hiring quotas. Another possible explanation is that the Labor Department has been lobbied hard by the National Association of Manufacturers and the AFL-CIO to resist changes in Executive Order 11246 and the administration wants to continue to make political gains among these constituencies.

The AFL-CIO and black congressmen have colluded to establish what are, in effect, quotas *against* black employment. The minimum wage law is one and the Davis-Bacon Act is another. The Davis-Bacon Act discriminates against non-union construction workers. Doing union bidding, black congressmen give unflinching support to the racially motivated Davis-Bacon Act.

There are literally hundreds of other laws and regulations whose modification or elimination would be far more effective in producing equal opportunity than the blind, mindless pursuit of racial quotas. Furthermore, the creation of freer markets (deregulation) would enhance black opportunities in racially non-divisive ways.

In the words of Robert Smalls, a black U.S. congressman from Beaufort, S.C. (1874-1886), "My race needs no special defense, for the past history of them in this country proves them to be the equal of any people anywhere. All they need is an equal chance in the battle of life."

The question is whether the Reagan administration has the moral courage to risk the alienation of powerful political forces to try to ensure that blacks have an equal chance in life. The courageous thing for Reagan to do is rescind Executive Order 11246 *and* order the Justice Department to initiate antitrust proceedings against hundreds of cruel laws that create special privileges for some Americans at the expense of other Americans.

December 1985

Stalking Horses

OLD WESTERN movies had bad guys creeping up on good guys by walking in step beside a horse so that they could get close enough for a good shot. Using stalking horses to disguise one's agenda is a pretty good idea. If discovered, the horse takes the first shot.

Blacks and poor people are frequently used as stalking horses to disguise the hidden agendas of all sorts of people. Affirmative action regulations were to "help" blacks, but the people who benefited were elite women and homosexuals. Food stamp programs were to help the poor, but striking union members and college students quickly cashed in. School lunch programs were to help poor kids, but now all kids, rich and poor, get the subsidy. There are many other examples of black and poor people being used for someone else's agenda.

Now people wishing to lace public schools with sex clinics have discovered a new use for blacks. Under the pretext of combatting high rates of teen pregnancy, Planned Parenthood and the Center for Population Options are heading the drive for high school sex clinics. According to a *Chicago Sun Times* report (9/15/85), the sex clinic at Chicago's DuSable High dispenses free birth control pills and condoms. Another clinic is scheduled to open February at another high school on Chicago's West Side. Not to be outdone, a high school in the predominantly black

Southwest area of Washington, D.C., will begin similar operations this year.

Students do need parental permission for the clinic's many services. Those services appear to be a pretext for what the clinics really want to administer—pregnancy testing, treatment of sex diseases, and prenatal and postpartum care. Judy Senderowitz, director of the D.C.-based Center for Populations Options, interviewed on a Washington talk show said that since other services are provided, when a kid walks into a clinic no one knows what service was received.

Sex clinics make a minor attempt to recognize parental authority. The consent form they use lists ten health services provided by the clinic such as emergency treatment, lab tests, and physical exams. The sex stuff is listed last, perhaps hoping parents won't notice.

The primary target of sex clinic operators is black schools. Using blacks to establish the "legitimacy" of a program now funded with private money and voluntary participation, they are going to get bolder. Yes, you've got it. Sex clinics will demand government funding and mandatory participation.

Parents should be concerned about this new turn of events. Many public schools have failed in what they're supposed to do—educate. This attempt to usurp more parental authority makes a stronger case for educational vouchers. Instead of states directly funding schools, each parent would get an educational voucher (something like the G.I. Bill). Parents would use vouchers to enroll their children in a school of their own choosing. Parents who don't want their fourteen-year-old children to receive condoms and pills would be able to choose a school without that policy.

What's amazing is that the liberal mentality that brings us high school sex clinics is the same liberal mentality of the sixties and seventies that told us, "Don't inhibit the kids," "Let it all hang out," and, "Do your own thing." It's like calling in the arsonist to put out the fire.

January 1986

Is Affirmative Action in Marriage Next?

IF I had any doubt that our legislators are long on wind and short on understanding, reading the editorial attack on Morris B. Abrams, vice chairman of the U.S. Civil Rights Commission, by Representatives Patricia Schroeder (D.-Colo.) and Olympia Snowe (R.-Me.) in a recent *New York Times* erased it. Abrams had said, "Comparable worth moves from the assertion of civil and political equality, which we all support, to economic and social equality, which many of us do not support." The two congresswomen called his statement ". . . utterly backward and entirely unsupportable."

Abrams' sin was the audacity to speak out against comparable worth. Well, just think about this: If comparable worth becomes law, judges would decide whether a truckdriver's job was of equal value to that of a secretary. And a judge could order the same pay be paid to each. The bureaucratic havoc that would heap on our economy would be beyond description.

In addition to the desire to place decision-making in the hands of an elite few, radical feminists support comparable worth because after years of laws and litigation differences in male-female median earnings remain. The feminist cliché is, "Women still earn 59 percent of the earnings of men." For people short on understanding, median income differences are an evil that must be corrected through congressional wisdom.

Let's look at other earnings differences. *Unmarried* men earn only 61 percent of the wages received on average by married men. *Black* female college graduates and professionals, as of 1970, earned incomes 25 percent greater than *white* female college graduates and professionals. Single female high school graduates who work continuously from age eighteen to thirty-seven earn slightly higher wages than males of the same description. As of 1973, never-married female college professors, with the same professional qualifications of their male counterparts, earned higher incomes.

When analyzing gender differences, it is not necessary to deny the existence of sex discrimination. But it is important to ask, "How much of what we see is attributable to it?" A key factor in the earnings capacity of women compared to men is marriage. When a man marries, he gets a *helper*. This means a man can bring work home, stay at work late, and not have it interfere with his husbandly obligations. This is less the case with women. Women give birth; men don't. Furthermore, it is the wife who is likely to take time off her job in the child's early years. She is also more likely to quit her job to accommodate her spouse's career advancement.

Marriage and children have opposite effects on male/female earnings. Married women earn less than unmarried women. Married women with children earn less than childless married women. On the other hand, married men earn more than single men, and married men with children earn more than married men without children.

Radical feminists not only ignore these differences, they insult married women. The fact that a man's name appears on a paycheck does not mean he alone produced it. His wife helped. This is suggested by the fact that married men earn more than their unmarried brothers.

I won't be surprised if tiny thinkers like Schroeder and Snowe call for affirmative action in marriage next.

January 1986

If Men Were Gods

GOD IS omnipresence, omniscience, and omnipotence. There are no restraints on God. Mere mortals are not gods. We must suffer ignorance, uncertainty, and weakness. The attempt to reduce the cost of these earthly burdens produces behavior that would be senseless if men were gods.

We pay an enormous price coping with ignorance. Billions of dollars are spent on advertising. We spend hours shopping for the best quality at the cheapest price. Real estate salesmen earn billions of commission dollars finding buyers for sellers. These activities would not exist if men were gods. Can you imagine a god spending hours shopping around for the best shoe bargain, or running in and out of houses with a real estate agent trying to find the best housing buy? A god would be spared this grief because of his all-knowingness.

Man's attempt to get information leads to all kinds of interesting behavior. Courtship is a fun activity, but it's also a search for information that helps one assess marital prospects. It is by no means a simple process; there are attempts to misrepresent data that have given rise to a multi-billion dollar plastic surgery and cosmetics industry to make people appear and smell as they are not.

One way we save on the cost of information is by stereotyping. We often assume that because a person has one physical characteristic of a group he also has its other characteristics. Young male drivers pay more for auto insurance than do young female drivers. Insurance companies expect higher claims from young males. For the same retirement premium, females get a lower benefit check. Why? Because insurance companies find females live longer than men. The National Organization for Women (NOW) screams foul. Why? Because not every young male is an aggressive driver and not every woman lives longer than every man.

NOW is right. But insurance companies don't know *which* person is the exception to the group. If God were in charge of insurance there'd be no such unfairness. He would not have to stereotype and discriminate. He would know which male was the higher accident risk and which women would live shorter lives, but we mortals must make do with inferior methods.

Civil rights spokesmen complain that the "ole boy" network of hiring discriminates against blacks. Whatever else the ole boy system may be, it's also a system for economizing on information costs. Under ole boy systems, a company seeks workers through word-of-mouth references from current employees, business acquaintances, or friends. The more important the job, the greater the role for ole boy networks.

Of course, if God were doing the hiring, there'd be no ole boy system. He would know the most suitable person for every job. We mortals must find a substitute for omniscience. When we hire a dentist to fix our teeth, we use the ole boy system. We ask a friend, "Do you know a good dentist?" Even black congressmen who condemn the ole boy system use it to hire friends, family, and acquaintances; have you ever seen an advertisement, "Congressional Legislative Assistant wanted?"

Just think how "fair" the world would be if only men were gods.

January 1986

Let Mikey Try It

I F YOU haven't tasted honey-dipped beetles before, what do you do? According to that cute cereal commercial, you let Mikey try it. One interpretation of that commercial is that Mikey is dispensable. If he barfs, no big thing, nothing's lost.

For nearly a generation, poor black people have played the role of society's Mikey. Politicians, scholars, civil rights leaders, you name it, have performed experiments—with no history of success—on blacks that hadn't been tried previously on anybody else.

Take racial quotas for the purposes of redressing historical grievances. There's no ethnic group in the world that can trace its upward socioeconomic progress to racial quotas. Jews, Japanese-Americans, Armenians, Italians, and West Indian American blacks (they were slaves), have faced racial discrimination. But the fact that they are now "successful" cannot be attributed to quotas either in employment or education.

We need not confine our attention to America. Chinese have faced discrimination in Southeast Asia; Indians in Africa; Jews in Europe; Armenians in the post-Ottoman Empire. But, for the most part, these ethnic groups earn higher income than those who discriminate against them.

Racial quotas to address grievances have been tried in India to help the Untouchables, and in Malaysia to help the dominant Malays who discriminate against the Chinese. Business set-asides and employment quotas have been tried. The bottom line in both places is failure to achieve the stated objectives.

During the 1960s and 1970s, it was frequently said that the problem of black education was the paucity of good black role models. That finding provided grist for the proposition that blacks should be put, by merit or by quota, into jobs as counselors, administrators, and school superintendents.

This has happened in some major cities, especially in the nation's capital, where you'll find a black school superintendent and numerous black principals and teachers. To boot, Washington's mayor and most of the city leaders and administrators are black. If the role-model theory were right, you'd expect Washington to be the mecca of black academic achievement. *Wrong.* The academic achievement of its black students is among the lowest in the nation.

American Jews have a reputation for academic achievement, but when poor, uneducated Jews migrated to New York, their teachers were Irish. Today, Japanese-Americans excel on most standards of academic achievement. But a Japanese student will wait a long time before he sees a Japanese role-model in school.

Politicians and civil rights leaders deride such jobs as washing dishes, delivering packages, and sweeping floors as one of the means for upward mobility. Yet most ethnic Americans got ahead by doing just that type of work. In fact, most of the blacks who deride "dead-end" jobs, and are now successful, at one time worked at those very jobs. So-called "dead-end" jobs teach people valuable work habits, such as promptness and respect for supervisors. What's more, a couple, both working at minimum-wage jobs, earns nearly $14,000 a year—well above the poverty level.

There are all kinds of experiments that people still want to perform on blacks. Before we let them proceed, we should ask, "Where has this idea worked before?" In a word, blacks need to be de-Mikeyfied.

August 1986

The "How Do You Know?" Problem

THE PURPOSE of racial quotas, according to all the good folks in the race business who would be out of jobs if America ever ran out of guilt, is to "redress past injustices by an unjust society."

They paint a one-dimensional picture, saying nothing of the moral, economic, and even psychological costs of distributing jobs and other social goodies by race. Some of these costs can be seen in the words, "How do you know?"

Today's quota policies raise real doubts in the eyes of many whites who wonder whether some blacks have *earned* their status, or whether they had it handed to them. Like sickle cell anemia, this "How do you know?" problem has become a sort of black man's disease.

It's not exclusively a black man's disease, however. Women and others who have been given special treatment also are victimized by it. Recently, I had the occasion to take a short commuter flight. Upon boarding the aircraft, I saw a woman sitting in the right hand side of the pilot's compartment. There I was, faced with the "How do you know?" problem, with pretty high stakes in the balance. My dilemma solved itself when I realized that the pilot sits on the left. My momentary panic—"How do I know whether she really knows how to fly this plane?"—was soon replaced by the nagging fear that this could be the flight where the pilot has a heart attack.

The "How do you know?" problem can affect white men too. Larry Bird, star player for pro basketball's Boston Celtics, has won the Most Valuable Player (MVP) Award the last two years. Between 1960 and 1984, the MVP was won by white players only twice. How do we know Larry Bird is really that good? Maybe Clarence Thomas, chairman of the Equal Employment Opportunity Commission, has ordered the National Basketball Association (NBA) to make the award to white players until their representation among MVP holders is equal to their representation in society? More realistically, how do we know the NBA hasn't made Bird into a hero in order to attract white fans to a sport dominated by blacks. Then again, maybe Larry Bird is that good, even though he's white. At six-feet-six, I'm an aging, but still pretty good, basketball player; I could check out Bird's credentials with a little one-on-one.

Then there is Chris Evert Lloyd and Martina Navratilova, who have dominated the women's tennis scene in recent years. Are they really that good? How do you know? Maybe Clarence Thomas should order Chrissy and Martina to take on male court stars Ivan Lendl and John McEnroe.

This "How do you know?" problem is vicious, demeaning, and spreading. Whenever a black moves into a position of high responsibility and leadership, he must confront the suspicion that he "made it" only because he's black—that a white man with the same credentials would still be fighting his way up the ladder.

The unhappy fact is that racial quotas help create racial antagonisms where they never existed. In New York City, for example, some policemen took and passed a reconstituted sergeants' examination only to have the results thrown out because the "right" number of blacks did not pass. Are you going to tell me some of them don't harbor racial feelings?

The real tragedy of all this is that racism and sexism in America could have died a natural death. Unfortunately, the race industry resuscitates it daily.

September 1986

45

Somebody Else's Agenda

IF THE Ku Klux Klan wanted to seriously sabotage black socio-economic mobility, they couldn't find better allies than liberal lawyers and judges, Planned Parenthood, and some government agencies and civil rights organizations. Let's look at the evidence.

The National Center for Neighborhood Enterprises promotes resident management of government housing projects. With some success, they try to eliminate the pathology and despair in these crime-infested places. The consensus of resident leaders is that Legal Services Corporation (LSC) lawyers are one of their main obstacles. When resident manager councils evict tenants who are drug pushers, pimps, and prostitutes, LSC lawyers come to their aid. Whose aid? You've got it—the drug peddlers, pimps, and prostitutes. The Ku Klux Klan would be warmed by this obstacle to black improvement.

In 1981, LSC lawyers filed suit on behalf of students challenging a Florida law requiring functional literacy as a requirement for high school graduation. According to LSC lawyers, it's unconstitutional for the state to require blacks to achieve the same level of literacy as whites. The Ku Klux Klan and other racists would choose the same strategy to sabotage black academic excellence.

The results of this nonsense lead to cases like *Smith, Sanders, et al.* v.

The University of Detroit Law School. Two black, female second-year law students with D+ grade averages were denied registration for the Fall 1983 semester because they failed to maintain a prescribed C grade average. The students alleged various discriminatory acts including the school's adoption of "grading techniques with the effect of disqualifying the lowest portion of the student body when it was apparent that blacks traditionally held the lowest levels of class standing."

The trial judge found no evidence of racial discrimination and dismissed the claim for damages but made a procedural error. Winning an appeal, on procedural grounds, the defendants were prepared for a lengthy court fight.

The Law School had already spent $185,000 in legal fees during the three-year life of this complaint; its insurance company urged an out of court settlement. Therefore, on September 23, 1986, the Law School paid the plaintiffs and their lawyers $60,000. The two black students got $20,000 and their two lawyers got $40,000.

The Klan would be pleased. Law schools seeking to avoid costly litigation will have greater incentive to pass unqualified black students. Other law schools thinking about outreach programs to help black students will be discouraged.

Then there's the Liberty City "Booby Trap Case" where Prentice Rasheed, after having been burglarized nine times, set a trap. He constructed an electrified wire net beneath his store's roof opening, the site of previous illegal entries.

Sure enough a burglar entered, was electrocuted, and died. Rasheed now faces prosecution for manslaughter; he violated the rights of the burglar.

The police will not and cannot protect black businessmen and residents. So what should black people do? Should they let criminals continue to turn their communities into economic wastelands? The Klan would like that.

In the next century, I wouldn't be surprised if every black person was a conservative. What would you expect from a people long victimized by liberals?

November 1986

Apartheid: American Style

MY RESEARCH shows that Afrikaner uniqueness is not found in the Afrikaner *desire* for apartheid, but in that apartheid is part of a legal structure enforced by South Africa's government.

While sheer racism can explain some of the pressure for apartheid, the evidence shows that economics plays the leading role. Let's take a tiny glimpse at the issue of apartheid.

In 1946, *Inspan,* an Afrikaner publication, said of South Africa's Indian merchants: "The one-time pitiful peddler has become a financially strong trader, whilst many hard-working established white businessmen have been squeezed out by the previously despised interloper." To defend Afrikaners, *Inspan* said, Afrikaner "businesses should be supported by their race." But these pleas fell on the deaf ears of Afrikaner customers whose racial solidarity came second to their desire for the cheaper prices and convenience of Indian stores.

Afrikaners who couldn't compete organized racist boycotts against Indian stores and became a significant part of the movement to have Indians sent back to India, which never materialized. For some reason, there was adherence to the 1912 agreement between Prime Minister Jan Smuts and Mohandas (later Mahatma) Gandhi not to forcefully repatriate Indians.

Afrikaners weren't alone in their contempt for Indian merchants. In 1949, bands of Zulus descended on Durban, burning and looting Indian shops. When the riot was over, 142 people lay dead and 1,087 wounded. Zulus thought that profits from stores in black areas should benefit their own people and not be taken away by Indian merchants. Zulus even told the government, "All we desire is that the government provide ships, and we will see the Indians on their way to India."

The same apartheid-type scenario is unfolding in some inner-city neighborhoods here in the U.S., where Vietnamese, Chinese, and Korean merchants are purchasing failing businesses and making a success of them, despite the staggering problems of crime, drugs, and prostitution that afflict these areas. For their efforts, these Asian merchants have received criticism and abuse from blacks, and sometimes whites, in cities like New York, Philadelphia, Los Angeles, Galveston, and Washington. In Washington, Korean merchants' stores have even been firebombed.

A most telling story is the on-going conflict between a Chinese merchant in Washington's Anacostia area and some of its black residents. The Rev. Willie Wilson of Union Temple Baptist Church demands the ouster of Asian merchants, saying, "We have been the stepping stones for so many businesses who come into the community, take all the money and resources out, and treat us bad." The Rev. Wilson said the picketing of Hung Chang Cheung's Good Hope Carry-out store, where Hung Chang Cheung, the owner, is alleged to have pulled a gun on a customer, will continue until the landlord rents to a black businessman.

South Africa solved its "problem" of Indian merchants being in areas "where they don't belong" by the 1950 Group Areas Act, which prohibits merchants of one race from setting up businesses in areas outside of their government-designated racial area. One wonders whether Willie Wilson and his followers would like to see similar legislation in Washington, or would they go the Zulu route—repatriate Asian merchants to the Far East?

Racism is despicable and worthy of condemnation, whether it's called apartheid or "keeping the money in the community."

December 1986

Chapter II

FREEDOM AND COERCION

THOMAS PAINE, in *Common Sense*, expressed the dilemma of government best: "Government, even in its best state, is but a necessary evil; in its worst state, an intolerable one." The essential characteristic of government is its power of coercion.

Man has not reached a state of grace where he no longer wishes to confiscate the property of his fellow man. In order to preserve personal liberty, we must have some organized institution to prevent one person from taking the property of another. Thus, one legitimate role of government is to provide a national defense (to prevent our foreign fellow man from confiscating our property) and a domestic defense (to prevent the same by our fellow countryman). Another is to provide mechanisms for enforcement of contracts and adjudication of disputes—that is, a judicial system. A reasonable case can be made that government should provide certain public goods that would not likely be privately produced, such as water projects, typhoid eradication, and highways, which the Framers had in mind when they said, "Congress shall provide for the general welfare."

The legitimate functions of government, of course, must be paid for. It is generally agreed that voluntary payments by citizens would not work; therefore, taxes are a legitimate way to finance government functions.

Today, most functions of United States federal, state, and local governments well exceed the scope of legitimacy. While there can be considerable debate over the definition of normative concepts like legitimacy, any reasonable interpretation must question the legitimacy of any government act where the property of one American is confiscated and given to another American to whom it does not belong. Nearly two-thirds of the federal budget consists of activities financed by confiscating the property of one American and giving it to another. The major government programs that fall into this category are: social security, agricultural and business subsidies, and welfare benefits. Any reader who believes confiscation is too strong a term to describe the government's acquisition of resources to pay for these programs should tell the Internal Revenue Service that he refuses to give up his earnings, and watch what happens.

Some people might argue that this confiscation is a result of "majority rule" and is legal and hence not theft. Then I would ask: How does something immoral, when done privately, become moral when it is done collectively? Furthermore, does legality establish morality? Slavery was legal; apartheid is legal; Stalinist, Nazi, and Maoist purges were legal. Clearly, the fact of legality does not justify these crimes. Legality, alone, cannot be the talisman of moral people.

The following columns examine some of the unintended side effects of coercion.

Greed Makes the World Go 'Round

W<small>HAT IS</small> the noblest of human motivations? Some would say love. Others would say courage. What about greed? The desire in each of us to have the things we enjoy is the motivation that creates the greatest good in the world. Many of you will be shocked at this exaltation of greed, so let me be more explicit: I support, encourage, and offer to abet, wherever possible, through legitimate means, human greed.

Look at New York City. Every single day there's meat delivered and available to Big Apple residents. Why? Is it because Texas ranchers love New Yorkers. You know it isn't; many Texans may even hate New Yorkers. But the ranchers are greedy. They want more for themselves. And this can best be accomplished by satisfying New Yorkers' needs with meat deliveries. Suppose meat deliveries to New York were made by the same people who deliver the mail? Well, we'd best not go into that.

Most of us have cars. Why? Is it because the corporate owners of Ford, General Motors, and Chrysler care about us personally? No way. They care mostly about themselves, but in the process *we* get what we want. We bet somewhere among the 240 million of us there's someone missing sleep trying to discover a 100-miles-per-gallon engine, a cure for herpes, or a way to teach computer language to illiterates. Can love for our fellow man explain *all* this effort? No, it's the desire to have more—greed.

Greed works miracles in other ways. I've often told people that I don't care that much about future generations. After all, what has a future generation person ever done for me? Some people are shocked, but then I explain what I do with my property. For example, several years back instead of buying a nice suit, which I could have had all to myself, I purchased ten two-year-old seedlings. Those trees will reach their maturation after I'm dead. I wasn't motivated out of love for future generations and a desire for them to have trees. I did it because the nicer my property, the higher the price I get when I sell it. Isn't that wonderful? By pursuing my own selfish interest I serve others. But I wouldn't have the same motivation if the government owned my house.

The important thing about greed is that for it to do you good, you must usually please others. The more you please others, the more you have for yourself. For example, there's an important please-the-people fight going on right now in computers. Apple is trying to out-please in order to beat out Atari, and IBM is trying to out-please them both. In fact, the richest people in the world are those who've done best at pleasing others, especially the common man. Computer companies are finding greater rewards by making computers for the common man. Henry Ford became richer than Bentley; Ford made cars for the common man.

Government-sponsored activity doesn't need wide appeal to survive. Take public broadcasting, who says it is listener-sponsored? That's a lie. I don't listen to it, but I sponsor it. Anyway, have you listened to its pleas for money? They are the most boring, tasteless commercials in the world, comprised of pleas for cash in exchange for a WGBH teddy bear. Give me a Brooke Shields commercial any day.

There's something about wealth accumulation that really bothers me, particularly around tax time. Very seldom does a week go by without some news media character, civil-rights zealot, or Tip O'Neill-type maligning the nation's more well-to-do citizens. Most of the well-to-do got that way because they worked hard and pleased more people than their competitors did. As a result of the pursuit of wealth, the high-earners pay higher taxes. I figure I support at least three families. Instead of malignment, people should thank me. You'd think that poor people who take some of my money would send me a 'thank you' card each year. My daughter, whom I also support, at least says, "Thank you, Daddy," once in a while.

April 1983

The Futures Market:
Classic Capitalism

Some of the most wonderful things are so common that they go virtually unnoticed and, for the most part, unappreciated. That's okay except for the fact that once in a while man, in his arrogance, thinks he can replace or improve on the natural order of things. For example, there are the wonders of free markets. It's important to consider these wonders, especially in light of the increasing verbal attacks on the "evils" of capitalism.

The summer of 1983 has been a devastating one for our agricultural sector. The melting of unusually late spring snow, coupled with rain, delayed planting. Then summer droughts destroyed crop after crop; some farmers lost 50 percent of their crop. Naturally, this means fewer vegetables, and since livestock feed on grains it will, in turn, reduce the number of chickens, cattle, and pigs available for the market.

Now the question is: Given the natural calamity down on the farm, what kinds of human action are consistent with the social good? There are several obvious actions we should take: (1) Consumers should economize on their use of farm products; (2) farmers should do their best to bring as much of their product to the market as they can (cutting down on wasteful harvesting methods); and (3) next year they should plant more to replace depleted stocks.

All of this sounds simple, but it's a tall order. If you think it's not, consider: There are thousands of farmers—how much land should Farmer Jones plant next year, and what should he plant? To cut down on food usage should Housewife Smith use more chicken and less pork, or more pork and less beef? And the wheat and corn we do harvest, how much of it should be used per month, and for what purpose? And, looking towards the next harvest, there is the dilemma of not knowing whether it will be a good or bad harvest.

For the most part, these questions, and a million more, are answered through the free market. In Chicago, there are exchanges known as the "futures" markets. These are centers where the myriad of speculators (guessers) interact. If they expect, say, a shortage of wheat in February, they buy February wheat contracts. The result is today's price of wheat rises because farmers are saving it for sale in February. The speculators guess, "I'll buy wheat now for $4.00 a bushel and make a handsome profit." Such activity makes more wheat available at a lower price in February than would otherwise be the case. But the speculator might guess wrong; he could have miscalculated the extent of crop loss which could result in a $3.00-a-bushel price in February. In that case he'd take a bath.

The housewife sees wheat product prices rise in September so she uses less by resorting to wheat substitutes. This causes more wheat to be available in February than would otherwise be the case if too much of it was used in September. Then, because this year's prices are higher, farmers will plan to plant more wheat next spring.

There are many parts to this scenario, but the wonder is that everybody does what's consistent with the social interest *without* coercion. Each person pursuing what he perceives to be in his own interests serves the social good.

Now, presto chango, a government bureaucrat takes over (as happened to help muddle the oil shortage). What incentives does a bureaucrat have, comparable to the speculator, to see to it there's the "right" amount of wheat available for February? Very little. The speculator will be wiped out if he guesses wrong or does not adjust to changing conditions; if the bureaucrat errs, he risks at most his job and none of his personal wealth.

Remember the coffee shortage several years back? Did you see empty coffee shelves and coffee lines? No. But with the gas shortage you experienced gas lines and gas stations with "No Gas" signs. But just because coffee isn't as "vital" as gas doesn't mean it's immune to lines. Those old enough to remember World War II and its food rationing remember coffee lines and empty coffee shelves.

The futures market is a classic case of capitalism. Before you let a bureaucrat or some other kind of interventionist tell you he can do better, make him prove it.

September 1983

Should There Be a Market in Vital Organs?

Over the last several months there have been several heart-rending news stories about organ transplants. Distraught relatives, in last-minute, desperate attempts to find critically needed organs, have appealed to congressmen, senators, and even the president to publicize their efforts. There's a better way to do this.

Today the decisions about transplants are left solely in the hands of the medical professionals. When a critically ill person needs an organ, doctors, through their communication network, seek a suitable donor. When a donor organ is found (which is no small task) doctors decide *who* gets it because there are more needy recipients than organs. We don't know the specific criteria doctors use to decide who among several compatible patients gets the organ, but we're sure it involves such criteria as: Whose turn is it or who needs it the most?

Why should that kind of criteria apply? Why should doctors make the decision? Are they gods? By way of comparison, should automakers decide who gets a car? Should farmers decide who gets food? Should construction workers decide who gets a house? In each of these cases the market decides. Namely, bucks decide who gets what. You might say that the market's not perfect, and I'd agree, but it surely beats, say, construction workers deciding who gets what kind of house.

I'd be willing to bet the rent money that a market would do a far superior job allocating organ transplants. More explicitly, I'm saying organs should be bought and sold. A market in organs would produce the right incentives on behalf of all participants. First, the seller, now called the donor, would have organs as a part of his estate. As such, he may have greater incentive to better care for himself. Conceivably, a good liver might fetch $100,000. Also, his heirs would be better off at his demise. With the prospect of getting $100,000 for a liver, you can bet the rent money that heirs would have considerable incentive to notify some sort of clearinghouse on the availability of a liver.

Second, recipients and their families can better decide whether it's worth it. As it is now, organs don't cost anything. That being the case, everybody sick thinks he *must* have one. I'm sure that if Rolls-Royces were zero-priced everyone requiring transportation would think he *must* have one. Since Rolls-Royces command a price, many people find they can do without one. Clearly, there are differences in "needs" for organs. Is a liver to a sick eighty-year-old patient as important as it is to a sick twenty-year-old? Or is it more important to a college graduate or a high school drop-out? Who can answer difficult questions like these, and why should the ultimate answer be left in the hands of doctors?

Now you say, "Who can afford $100,000?" There are a lot of things that cost $100,000 and more. That's why there are mortgage markets that give loans for houses, yachts, college educations—and now, why not livers?

Some might object to all of this by saying that to establish a market for organs is difficult. Difficult is not the same as impossible. Others might question the morality of selling organs. Well, whatever is yours you have the right to sell. The major opponents to this proposal—to buy and sell organs—would be the medical professionals. Their arguments probably would center around "ethical" issues, but the real reason is a market in organs would take power from them and put it in the hands of the people.

April 1984

Defining Social Justice

THE WHOLE debate over what government should be doing, what programs it should sponsor, and how much it should tax and spend has been shallow at best. The Reagan administration which *says* it wants to cut spending, taxing, and government controls has been portrayed as simplistic, mean, and uncaring. But nobody in the White House knows, or has the guts to talk about, the legitimate role of government in a free society. And sadly enough, only a few congressmen, most notably Ron Paul (R.-Tex.) and Robert Walker (R.-Pa.), both understand and have the guts to argue the case for individual liberty and limited government.

At the heart of the question about the legitimate role of government is another question: What kind of social order do we want? This columnist believes that on balance most Americans prefer relationships which are voluntary and non-coercive. That means most Americans prefer exchanges like, "I'll do something good for you if you do something good for me." The reason is both parties benefit. That's the essence of your relationship with the painter, butcher, and gasoline station owner. You do something good for him—pay money—and he does something good for you—deliver the product. It's all voluntary.

By contrast our relationships with government are mostly coercive. You *must* pay, through taxes, for Amtrak, crop irrigation, food stamps, the International Monetary Fund, foreign aid, the United Nations, and $800-billion-plus worth of other things whether you receive the service or not, and whether you like it or not. You pay—or you go to jail. The nature of government is coercion. Government, however, is a necessary evil. There must be some bit of government coercion to prevent others, foreign and domestic, from taking that which belong to us—our rights and our lives. To finance the legitimate government functions there must be taxes to support the military and police. There are disputes at law and contracts which suggest a role for government in adjudication. There may be one or two other legitimate functions for government in a free society, but not many more. And surely government shouldn't be in the business of taking from one and giving to another.

Most government activity is what mathematicians call "zero-sum," where one person gains *only* at the expense of another. For example, when government gives one American one dollar, some other American *must* be worse off by *at least* one dollar plus the handling charges for some bureaucrat to broker the transaction. Or when Reagan helped Harley-Davidson by putting tariffs on Honda bikes, the company gained; but American bike consumers lost through being forced to pay higher prices.

Because government interference involves coercion, there is a moral reason for limited government.

There are some Americans, however, who like government activity since it allows them to do things they cannot do when relationships are voluntary. Chase Manhattan Bank officers like government intervention because they suspect we won't voluntarily help bail them out for making imprudent loans. So they get government to confiscate our money to help bail them out. Sol Chaiken, president of the International Ladies' Garment Workers Union, can't get us to voluntarily buy higher priced shirts made by his high-wage members. So he gets government to keep Hong Kong-made shirts out so we'll be forced to buy the more expensive, union-made shirt or do without. Do-gooders figure we won't voluntarily give enough money to feed poor people plus pay for the do-gooders' limousines: So they get government to confiscate our money through taxation.

Each of these activities constitutes illegitimate government activity. They are totalitarian acts veiled by modern names like "welfare," "industrial policy," and "orderly markets," but this can't hide the fact that these are totalitarian acts nonetheless.

Government growth and control is inconsistent with a free and prospering society.

But you might say, if government didn't do all that it's doing we wouldn't have a *just* society. What's *just* has been debated for centuries but let me offer my definition of social justice: I keep what I earn and you keep what you earn. Do you disagree? Well then tell me how much of what I earn *belongs* to you—and why?

January 1984

Scientific Dishonesty

THE MONT Pelerin Society, an international organization of economists and other scientists who cherish limited government and personal liberty, held its general meeting this month in Cambridge, England. This august body's membership includes Nobel Laureates like Milton Friedman, George Stigler, and its founder Friedrich von Hayek. Other distinguished members include: Professors Henri Lepage, Karl Brunner, Chiaki Nishiyama, and James Buchanan, the next likely American Nobel Laureate in Economics.

Usually we spend a week listening to papers on various ways government is used to restrict personal liberty. This year there was a variation on that theme in the session: "The Abuse of Science in Public Policy." The major paper was delivered by Edith Efron, author of *The Apocalyptics: Cancer and the Big Lie* (Simon & Schuster, 1984). The thrust of Efron's paper and her book is that people have used public fear of cancer to enhance government control over our lives. She points out that the big lie starts with such assertions as, "Industrially produced chemicals and products account for 90 percent of cancer deaths since World War II." With no supporting evidence, major television, print, and radio news sources harangue us about the man-made cancer epidemic; we are told, Nature is good and Man is evil, especially those men in the Fortune 500.

The fact is cancer didn't start after World War II. According to research at the University of Zurich, dinosaurs, 200 million years ago, were found to have osteoma and osteosarcoma. Mummies dating from the pre-Columbian times have been found with osteosarcoma and multiple myeloma. Surely Dow Chemical and Exxon weren't responsible for this suffering.

Simple, honest scientific inquiry reveals *nature* is the earth's major carcinogenic agent. There are literally thousands of natural carcinogens which include solar, galactic, and terrestrial radiation, minerals, volcanic aerosols, viruses, bacteria, fungi, plants, and trees. Our daily diet of proteins, cholesterol, sugars, salt, and hydrocarbons contains cancer-causing materials. Carcinogens can't be avoided. Not even Congress can eliminate volcanoes and solar radiation.

But Congress can make things worse. Based on a faulty study and public panic, EDB (ethylene dibromide), a grain fumigant, has been outlawed. Interestingly enough, the EDB ban remains in force despite the fact the Environmental Protection Agency (EPA) found the report faulty. According to a paper presented by William Havender, the government has mandated the use of EDB substitutes that are known carcinogens, that are not tested, and may be a higher cancer risk than the highly tested EDB.

This is typical for Congress. Remember the cyclamate, saccharin, and sodium nitrite issues? These false scares were based on what the American Statistical Association and Society of Toxicologists referred to as creative statistics "foreign to everything that is taught in the statistics profession."

Of course the point of scientific dishonesty is to trick the public into supporting billions of dollars of research programs and to create multi-billion dollar government agencies to "protect" us from cancer. But, as usual, you can't blame the politicians, bureaucrats, and environmentalists, for the pack consists of many running dogs including the target of these attacks—business. For example, guess who lobbied against cyclamates being recertified by the Food and Drug Administration? None other than the manufacturers of Nutrasweet. And guess who lobbies against the use of Western non-union coal as a health hazard? Eastern unionized coal producers.

Scientific quackery has been used to justify Marxism, racism, and all kinds of persecution. Now it's being used to justify bigger government.

September 1984

Invisible Victims of
High Tariffs

THE SADDEST fact of life is we can't get something for nothing. Every benefit carries a price tag. Politicians try to convince us otherwise, and often succeed because the victims of their efforts are invisible. But economists are faced with the "dismal" task of revealing the truth: Every benefit has a cost.

The U.S. steel industry has problems surviving in a highly competitive world market. And Walter Mondale promises the steelworkers' union that, if he is elected, tariffs will be imposed on foreign steel to give our decaying domestic industry "some breathing room." The obvious benefit is to promote employment in the steel industry.

Because low-price foreign steel is being purchased by manufacturers of steel products, domestic producers cannot sell enough steel at current prices to sustain current wages and still earn a normal rate of return on investment. Tariffs will drive the price of foreign steel up to a price equal to or higher than domestic steel, so manufacturers of steel products will buy American steel. Employment and profits will rise in the domestic steel industry. That's the benefit side.

Unfortunately, there is also a cost side. Manufacturers of steel-using products face higher input prices. One effect is to raise the price of such goods as autos, washing machines, and filing cabinets. If these goods cost more, consumers buy fewer of them. That results in reduced employment in those industries. So the tariff on foreign steel shifts unemployment from the steel industry to some other industry.

And let's look at another side effect: What do Korean steel exporters do with the dollars they earn by selling us steel? U.S. dollars can change hands many times around the world, but ultimately they are good only in the U.S. If foreigners have fewer dollars as a result of selling less steel to the U.S., they will buy fewer U.S. products. For example, they may have been buying U.S. lumber products. With fewer dollars they will buy less lumber, which reduces employment in that industry. Again, tariffs shift unemployment, perhaps causing more jobs lost than gained.

For politicians this is great. They can give a benefit to one political constituency and avoid blame for the cost; virtually no one connects higher employment for steelworkers and less employment somewhere else.

I can't think of a reason, but there *may* be some justification for protecting inefficient U.S. companies. But the costs should be kept honest and aboveboard. One way is for the companies and their unions to come to Washington. If they need a $3 billion subsidy to survive each year, they should ask Congress to vote for Aid to Dependent Steel Companies legislation. That way the subsidy is made public.

Steelworkers are more privileged than most Americans and their foreign counterparts. In 1980, Japanese and German steelworkers earned $8.50 an hour, about what the average American manufacturing laborer gets. Because of a powerful union, as opposed to productivity, American steelworkers get more than double that wage.

Countering Mondale's tariff scheme is the Reagan administration proposal to solve the problem through "voluntary restraints." This isn't in the best interests of Americans either; it's just not as bad as the Mondale plan.

October 1984

The Sky Didn't Fall

"AIRLINE DEREGULATION will cause small communities to lose air service, cause a reduction in safety standards, jeopardize jobs, and threaten carriers with bankruptcy." That's the kind of wild assertion that was made during the airline deregulation debate. No less a personage than columnist George F. Will whimpered in *The Washington Post* (1/27/77), "But profit-maximizing freedom also might lead to abandonment of service to many communities."

Now that we've had several years of partial deregulation we can reflect on those predictions that the market wouldn't work and that without big brother the sky might fall.

In 1978, small commuter airlines flew, according to a *USA Today* (10/4/84) report, about 11 million passengers per year. By the end of 1983 they were carrying nearly 22 million passengers a year. The Regional Airline Association predicts that by 1993 there will be 65 million commuter airline travelers. There are 250 airlines providing services to out-of-the-way places like Boone, North Carolina, Lake Jackson, Texas, and Paducah, Kentucky, accommodating their schedules to those of major carriers. These are the places, according to pre-deregulation rhetoric, that were supposed to be cut off from the air travel mainstream of American society.

Airline deregulation didn't produce wholesale community abandonment by air services, nor did it produce a rash of air crashes. But it did bring bankruptcies and reorganization—and for good reason.

Deregulation (or market competition) *does not* mean businessmen can do as they please. Very much to the contrary, free-market competition is the most stringent, unyielding form of regulation there can be. That's precisely why so many sellers fear and abhor the free market; and airline companies are no exception. Under free-market competition, survivors are those who provide the most satisfactory service judged by an unyielding pressure group—the customers.

If an airline is providing poor-quality service at high cost, free markets mean a competitor can enter to vie for the customer. But under government regulation, airlines can use government to keep the competition out via route monopolies. Or if a competitor can provide the same service but at a lower cost, the incumbent airline can get government to fix fares so the new entrant cannot charge lower prices to attract customers.

Not only does airline management like regulation, airline unions love it as well. The reason? They can demand wages and work agreements out of line with their productivity. Managers can have a cozy relationship with unions because they only need to apply to government regulators for a fare increase to cover the higher costs. However, under free-market competition, if one airline pays its pilots $100,000 a year and another airline finds it can hire pilots for $40,000 a year, guess who's going to be in financial trouble and guess which pilot will support regulation? And while we're at it, take a guess at which arrangement will mean higher fares?

In an unusual show of editorial brilliance, *The Washington Post* (4/9/77) saw through the self-serving anti-deregulation rhetoric, "This desire for a system of government regulation that permits you to be successful and keeps you from being unsuccessful is rather common these days." That astute observation applies to *any* seller, whether it's Ford Motors selling cars, U.S. Steel hawking steel, or the unions selling labor. Their common desire is to use government to lock out potential competitors—whether by import tariffs, "voluntary restraint," minimum wages, or airline regulation.

October 1984

Unconstitutional Conventions

THE U.S. Supreme Court seems to be confused over its constitutional powers. In fact, it should be charged with contempt of the U.S. Constitution. This ignoble status wasn't achieved through appointments to the court by any recent president; it's evolved through an insidious process spanning several decades, starting in the 1930s when the court broke with its tradition of judicial review of economic matters.

President Franklin Roosevelt was pressing his interventionist domestic economic policy only to have the Supreme Court declare it unconstitutional. So Roosevelt tried to "pack" the court with six additional justices who'd rule in favor of his social programs. But court-packing became unnecessary when Justice Owen Roberts switched his vote to a position satisfactory to the New Dealers.

The long reign of court constitutional terror began with its complete abandonment of *substantive* interpretation of the due process clauses of the Fifth and Fourteenth Amendments. This was replaced by *procedural* interpretation. Essentially, the court used to judge whether government economic interferences ignored individual freedom and the right to contract. Today's court is no longer influenced by such "trivia." All they want to know is whether government interference is *procedurally* sound, which means: Was there notice, was it capricious or discriminatory, and was there a right to a hearing? The pre-switch court would have (as it in fact did) thrown out the minimum wage law on constitutional grounds. Mercantilist occupational and business licensure laws were thrown out on the same constitutional grounds.

And the court has overstepped its constitutional limits in other ways, most notably by ignoring the Tenth Amendment which says, "The powers not delegated to the United States by the Constitution, nor prohibited by it to the States, are reserved to the States respectively, or to the people." This is the "states-rights" feature of our Constitution which served as a refuge for racists during the civil rights struggle. But the amendment also means the federal government *cannot* establish a local police force, mandate a 55-mph speed limit, or constitutionally interfere in state and local matters.

If you read court opinions, you'll note the teeth-grinding and hand-wringing attempts by the justices to reinterpret the intentions of the framers of our Constitution. Their behavior is as enlightened as that of the ancient scholastics who argued over how many teeth were in a horse's mouth, instead of getting up off their butts, going to the barn, looking in a horse's mouth, and counting the teeth. The framers made it patently clear what they meant when they adopted the Constitution. The justices—and any American—need merely read *The Federalist Papers,* which were written by Constitution drafters Alexander Hamilton, John Jay, and James Madison. The justices can't be that ignorant. They, more than anyone else, know precisely what the Constitution means. Yet they conduct their own private mini-constitutional conventions in their chambers.

Want proof? In 1984, the court ruled in *Hawaii Housing Authority* v. *Midkiff* that the State of Hawaii could, through right of eminent domain, confiscate private property, not for public but for private use. A large percentage of the land in the Aloha State is owned by five or six families who lease it to tenants. The court ruled that the state could take this land, giving the owners what the state deemed was a fair price, and, in turn, sell it to others. That is the court's largest, recent raid on private property.

I have been flattered by offers of cabinet-level appointments. I've turned them down. I'm afraid I would embarrass the president with my unyielding love of freedom. But, I will accept, without reservation, an appointment to the U.S. Supreme Court. Now you might say, "Walter, you're not a lawyer!" Well, the Constitution *doesn't* require a supreme court justice to be a lawyer. Maybe its framers were trying to tell us something?

December 1984

Why Do We Pay the Price?

How many times have you wanted to get on a bus only to find you *must* have the "exact change?" And how about police warnings not to have your address visible on your luggage? Or the lengthy warnings to the kids regarding child molestation? How about inner-city residents having to trek out to the affluent suburbs to shop? And finally, how about having to register at the principal's office before visiting your child's teacher, then having to pass several police officers on the way to the class.

These and many other precautions are a part of living safely in many areas in modern America. Those over forty years old will remember that today's myriad of precautions for personal security were not a part of their growing up. The only policeman they saw in their school was "Officer Friendly," the public relations program officer used to help kids relate to law enforcement.

The day-to-day crime precautions we take today are not free. They cost us in terms of money, inconvenience, and a lower quality of life. Stores must charge higher prices to make up for both customer and employee theft. And where thefts are too high, stores move out. Then residents in those areas must board buses, subways, or trains, or drive long distances to suburban malls to shop. In some neighborhoods, Chinese restaurants, clothing cleaners, and other establishments must serve customers through a hole in the wall because of all the robberies. All this adversely affects the quality of life.

This is neither an act of God nor a mystery. It is a result of generalized contempt for the safety of honest citizens by the courts, the penal institutions, and the legal profession. In the name of half-baked sociological theories and perverted ideas of justice, criminals have been given *carte blanche* to prey on society—on you and me.

And while crime affects us all, no one bears the burden as much as poor people. Robert Woodson, director of the National Center for Neighborhood Enterprise, describes several important efforts by public housing residents to upgrade their living standards. In many instances, to accomplish this requires that property managers evict drug pushers and prostitutes. But the ACLU or legal aid lawyers go to court to have the eviction voided. With that kind of morale boost it's not hard to understand how criminals are emboldened to try anything from rape and murder to holdups on buses and trains. For the middle-class there is an escape—to better neighborhoods. But for the poor there is none.

What's the solution? The answer is more citizen participation. At the political level, we can force politicians to either adopt strong law enforcement measures or be voted out of office. This is especially effective at the local level. Citizens can form private organizations to monitor judges and parole boards, to publicize the names of judges who give criminals light sentences and those "do-gooders" on parole boards who set them free. We have Neighborhood Watch; now we need Judge and Parole Board Watch. If manufacturers can be sued for defective products, we should be able to sue the court system for defective protection.

Since the legal establishment seems to be on the side of criminals we may have to resort to private protection. The Guardian Angels, who patrol the streets, buses, and subways of cities like New York, are a worthwhile example. But what a man did in New York City several weeks ago is another. Four thugs threatened him, so he shot and wounded the whole lot. Now the police have a manhunt out for the "Death Wish" killer; but New York's citizens have been calling the police praising him as a hero.

One way or another, criminals, the police, judges, and parole boards must learn that the American people—the victims of rampant criminals—are fed up.

January 1985

Balance of Payments Deficit

MOST PUBLIC statements regarding our balance-of-payments deficits are throwbacks to the Middle Ages' mercantilist theory that prosperity requires exports to equal or exceed imports, otherwise the country's gold must pay for the excess imports, making the country poorer. According to mercantilist theory, the wealth of a nation is its gold and silver.

Adam Smith challenged this in *An Inquiry Into the Nature and Causes of the Wealth of Nations. The Wealth of Nations,* its short title, came out in 1776 and became an important part of early America. Smith proved that the wealth of nations consists of their annual production and consumption, *not* the quantity of gold and silver they possess.

According to Smith, ". . . foreign trade . . . carries out that surplus part of the produce of their land and labour for which there is no demand among them, and brings back in return for it something else for which there is demand . . . something else that may satisfy part of their wants, and increase their enjoyment."

This means that if a Honda brings you satisfaction, you pay its Japanese Producer $6000 and he delivers your car. So far there's no trade imbalance. You have $6000 worth of car; he has $6000 cash. People panic over a trade imbalance thinking merely that you wind up owning a

73

car and Japan owns dollars. This does create an imbalance of the *current* account, but there is an overall balance in the sense of value. The Japanese, instead of taking $6000 worth of physical goods, took claims to future goods. They hold onto these claims in the forms of Treasury bonds and other financial assets, like AT&T or IBM stock. What's wrong with foreign investment in the United States? That's part of what made us rich in the first place; people love having a safe, stable source of investment.

Thanks to our economic vitality, the dollar is strong relative to most currencies. Quite simply that means foreigners, especially the British, are willing to part with many units of their currency in exchange for a unit of ours. The result is lower prices for their goods relative to ours. And Americans love less expensive clothing, clocks, television sets, radios, and the like. We also like lower prices for hotels, meals, and entertainment. That's why so many more Americans find European vacations attractive now. Tourism is another form of foreign trade.

Who can be against less expensive trade goods? You've got it. The businessmen and unions, and the congressmen who represent them. They would like to prevent you from purchasing less expensive foreign products so they can charge higher prices. Labor unions know that if businessmen can increase prices, the unions can hit up the bosses for higher wages. So it's easy to see why these two groups scream the loudest about the flood of imports. Predictably, I have not heard a single consumer cry about low-cost imports. Free trade is one of the most pro-consumer deals going.

Regarding low-cost imports, you'll hear nonsense from the likes of Chrysler President Lee Iacocca and union boss Lane Kirkland, such as: "I believe in free trade, but fair trade." This shibboleth refers to the fact that other countries restrict imports. They urge us to do the same. What they urge differs little from saying America shall not be free until other countries allow their citizens to be free. Nonsense!

Americans shouldn't be frightened into unwise trade restrictions by the trade deficit rhetoric. The "trade deficit" can become a problem if foreigners suddenly withdraw their dollars. But as long as we maintain a robust, stable, and growing economy there will be no *en masse* exit of dollars.

February 1985

Did You Vote for This?

Q UITE OFTEN this writer's criticism of government evokes the cliché, "We live in a democratic society and elected representatives do what the people want." Even if this were true, it's not the test of freedom, for most of what we do shouldn't be decided by a vote. Whether you're going to live in Texas or California, own a foreign car or a domestic one, or eat oranges or apples are decisions that shouldn't be decided by a ballot.

But let's talk about the hanky-panky done to us by the people we vote into office. A new organization, Citizens for a Sound Economy (CSE), recently surfaced in Washington, D.C. From all that I can tell, they've taken on the responsibility of exposing congressional lies, theft, and a host of things that would lead to arrest for the ordinary citizen.

CSE's latest report is on the U.S. Department of Agriculture's little-known marketing orders. Marketing order regulations affect some fifty different fruits, vegetables, and specialty crops. These edicts regulate matters like advertising, joint research, production control, and the sale and distribution of farm products. In short, they constitute a government-sponsored cartel.

One of the most flagrant examples of congressionally sponsored cartels is the Navel Orange Administrative Committee. Congress allows this committee to determine the percentage of the navel orange crop that can be sold fresh. The rest of the harvest, normally 30 to 40 percent of what's grown, must, by law, either be left to rot or sold as byproducts or cattle feed for a pittance—sometimes around $10 a ton. Several years ago, you may have seen the NBC feature showing mountains of California navel oranges rotting.

Now why would anyone want oranges kept off the market? You got it! The smaller the available supply, the higher the price charged. So who's behind the game? A major player is Sunkist. The marketing order system favors large cooperatives like Sunkist. Sunkist's Washington lobbyists fight tooth and nail to retain the marketing order system that enriches them at the expense of the general consumer. And look at the power they have. Several years ago the Federal Trade Commission (FTC) just talked about doing a study of marketing orders with an eye toward bringing an anti-trust suit. Sunkist lobbyists, as well as many others, descended on Congress like a horde of angry hornets. The result: Congress mandated that the FTC could conduct *no* studies of marketing orders. Furthermore, if any FTC commissioner, in his official capacity, said anything about marketing orders he risked imprisonment.

Last year's crop freeze in Florida led to Agriculture Secretary Block's suspension of the pro-rate system of orange marketing orders. Orange prices fell as much as 30 percent and consumers ate 130 million more pounds than they did when the orange cartel controlled output.

The White House is now being pressured to re-regulate oranges. The cartelizers are being led by that man with the greatest concern for the poor and hungry in America, that staunch consumer advocate Sen. Alan Cranston (D.-Calif.). With help like that, if I'm in a fight with a bear, I want Cranston to help the bear.

Does the average consumer want his congressman to vote for higher fruit and vegetable prices? The answer's quite probably no. Then why do congressmen do it? It's all part of the same game: Congressmen use their office to create advantages for one American at the expense of another. If Citizens for a Sound Economy can't stop the game they're going to at least let us know when—and how—it's being played.

July 1985

Hold On to Your Wallet

MAN'S SEARCH for something-for-nothing has always proved unsuccessful. This does not mean the search is over. Some in Congress are still trying to repeal, amend, or modify the laws of Mother Nature, and at least give the impression of creating something-for-nothing. But what their hocus-pocus is more likely to create are problems even bigger than the ones they are trying to solve.

Consider the free trade issue. Congress has returned to Washington with a vengeance, and with a rush to enact tough foreign trade legislation to protect American jobs and industry from "unfair" foreign competition. Some Americans see such help as free—since it does not add to the federal budget—and thus, *presto magico,* Congress has created something for nothing. But don't believe that. And hold on to your wallet.

Let's go through a small step-by-step examination of the problem, using the American shoe industry as an example. Since 1970, the American shoe industry has "lost" some 95,000 jobs. Today, another 30,000 jobs are threatened. But why the decline?

When U.S. consumers shop for shoes, most will choose the less expensive shoe over the same shoe that costs more. The bad news for

U.S. footwear manufacturers is that shoes from Korea, Taiwan, or Italy are often less expensive than those made domestically. Therefore, the consumer who chooses the less expensive foreign shoe over the domestic manufacturer's product has created a problem for the U.S. producers.

In free societies, of course, there's nothing wrong with individuals deciding one shoe is more of a bargain than another; who can be against that kind of freedom? Well, the domestic shoe manufacturers and their workers are against it. They want you to buy their products.

They could lure you by lowering their prices. However, that might mean lower profits and wages. And they don't want any part of that bitter pill.

So they appeal to Congress to enact legislation to restrict your choices. Their armies of lobbyists pressure Congress to reduce shoe imports through quotas and tariffs. Quotas place numerical limits on imports and reduce your selection of shoes; tariffs raise the price of imports and make foreign shoes less of a good buy.

Had President Reagan caved in to the recent shoe lobby effort, 240 million American consumers would have been forced to pay an estimated $15 billion more each year in higher shoe prices. That sleight-of-hand $15 billion handout to the shoe industry would not have shown up as a government expenditure, but it surely would have had the full effect of a tax on the public. Congressmen like handing out these kinds of favors, because few people make the connection between tariffs and quotas and the higher prices they end up paying.

One of the tragedies of trade restrictions is that they are actually more costly than the 'buddy-can-you-spare-a-dime' type of handout. Shoe import restrictions would have saved 30,000 jobs at a cost to consumers, in higher shoe prices, of $15 billion a year. That means it would have cost the public $50,000 for every job saved. But guess what? The average salary of U.S. shoe workers is around $14,000. Only in Washington is it sensible to spend $50,000 to save $14,000—sensible because it's somebody else's money.

There is nothing sacred about the shoe industry. Some U.S. industries decline as a part of the natural technological evolutionary process. Others decline because federal tax, labor, and clean air laws handicap them, and make them less able to compete. After all, the IRS, OSHA, and EPA have no jurisdiction in Korea, Taiwan, and Hong Kong.

The special-interest pleading of the shoe industry is only the tip of the iceberg on the 99th Congress's fall agenda. Special pleadings also are coming from the textile, auto, steel, and electronics industries. One thing is clear: If your congressman votes for a free lunch for any one of these industries, you know who'll pick up the tab. And it isn't Mother Nature.

September 1985

How Do We Know
What's Fair?

W<small>E CAN</small> hardly get through a day without hearing someone sounding off about something being "unfair." "It's unfair that some people (or countries) are rich while others are poor." "It's unfair that women on the average earn less than men." Jesse Jackson will tell you it's unfair that blacks are under-represented in executive positions. Ralph Nader tells us big corporations and corporate takeovers are unfair.

Mankind has been debating what's fair for centuries and there's still no consensus. Part of the problem is that fairness, like beauty, is in the eye of the beholder. Science knows of no way to establish the correctness of subjective statements. After all, if someone says anchovies are delicious and you say they aren't, there's no way to establish who's right. However, objective statements, such as "hydrogen is lighter than lead," can be scientifically tested for correctness.

But hard as it is to evaluate what's fair, we must try, because our Bill of Rights, liability laws, election system, customs, mores, and laws, are all rooted in some assumption of "What's fair?"

Much of the confusion comes from our temptation to emphasize *results* while downplaying *process*. Take a game like poker. We cannot tell from the results whether the game is fair. The fact that Smith loses 80 percent of the time, while Jones wins 80 percent of the time cannot tell us whether the game is fair. Jones might just be better at the game, or maybe he's cheating; but nothing about fairness can be determined by studying the results.

Take the following example: Blacks comprise 12 percent of the population; however, more than 75 percent of professional basketball players are black, and they are the highest paid. Is that fair? Surely, just knowing the results, or the way things are, can't answer that question. We have to look at the process, or how things got that way. Did someone prevent other ethnic groups from competing? Is there government-backed collusion among team owners? Or are blacks just better? Civil rights leaders ignore process; they base their policy on results. With such a view it would be natural for them to call for racial quotas for white and Oriental basketball players.

Hardly a month goes by without the media or some politician attacking some form of income. They attack the fact that some group earns a lot of money or that some corporation earns "obscene" profits. Just looking at a result such as earnings leads to the politics of demagoguery and envy. We must look at process; why do some people earn more than others? Most earnings are a result of man pleasing his fellow man. Your babysitter earns money by pleasing you by taking good care of the kids. You earn money by pleasing your employer. IBM earns money from pleasing us all. Michael Jackson earns more than Pavarotti because he pleases more people. Chrysler, some years ago, lost a lot of money by not pleasing enough people.

If we see people voluntarily buying IBM products, or Michael Jackson's videos, and there are no restraints on competitors such as Apple, Kaypro, or Pavarotti, the profits are fair. Chrysler made profits; but those profits are not all the result of serving the public well. They are in part due to Chrysler's successfully wheedling the federal government to reduce competition by imposing limits on Japanese imports. In that sense, Chrysler's profits can be described as obscene.

Fairness cannot be determined by the way things are. We must look at how things got that way, and there's a pretty good rule for this. Generally, if outcomes are a result of voluntary exchange, they're fair. If they are a result of force, they are unfair.

October, 1985

The Catholic Bishops Ride Again

LED BY Archbishop Rembert Weakland, the Catholic bishops delivered their second draft of "Catholic Social Teaching and the U.S. Economy." The second draft is just like the first, steeped in misunderstanding and immorality. The bishops don't intend to be ignorant and immoral, but their words tell the tale.

The bishops wonder, ". . . [D]oes our system place more emphasis on maximizing profits than on meeting human needs and the fostering of human dignity?"

Contrary to the bishops' pretense, there's little conflict between profit and human needs. In fact, the pursuit of profits is the activity *most* consistent with meeting human needs; we just never really give it a thought. Just think, New Yorkers need meat and potatoes. Their needs are not met because Texas ranchers and Idaho farmers feel Christian warmth towards them. They're met because Texans and Idahoans love profits.

But profit is a two-edged sword. To maximize it not only must human needs be satisfied, they must be satisfied in a way that economizes on the world's scarce resources. Thus, profit maximization requires satisfaction of needs at the lowest cost. The same principle applies to the millions of other human wants and needs, ranging from computer chips and antibiotics to Barbie dolls and designer jeans.

The bishops' immorality is seen in their attack on private property. They say, "No one is justified in keeping for his exclusive use what he does not need, when others lack necessities." However, in the face of others' lacking necessities, the bishops don't say what qualifies as things you do not need. Do you need a Cadillac? Or can you make do with a Pinto? Do your kids really need expensive Christmas toys while other kids are starving in Africa? Do you need two television sets in your house, or can you make do with one or none? Or do the bishops need to dine at the exclusive Tiberio Ristorante?

What if you don't voluntarily give up things the bishops say you don't need, what would be the course of action prescribed? Since the bishops don't have an army, they would call for government to confiscate what you don't need. That is, the government would take part of your pay before you see it—saving you from spending it on *unnecessary* things.

This brings us to the true tragedy of the bishops' message. They claim they're not calling for socialism, but that is precisely what they are doing. The tragedy and human suffering of socialism is visible all over the world. Indeed, one of the great untold stories is the strong connection between Germany's Naziism (which stands for National Socialist German Workers' Party) and socialism. Fichte, Rodbertus, Lensch, and Lassalle were not only the ancestors of Naziism; they are also acknowledged fathers of socialism.

Most people like to think the horrors of World War II were the result of madman Hitler at Germany's helm. Nonsense. A considerable part of what we saw in Germany was the attempt to make socialism work.

Lensch said, "Socialism must present a conscious and determined opposition to individualism." Hitler's expression of Nazi philosophy is, "gemeinnutz geht vor Eigennutz." (The common good comes before the private good). The bishops' Pastoral Letter expresses the same sentiment, "It is the very essence of social justice to demand from each individual all that is necessary for the common good."

In free societies, the only legitimate function of government is to preserve and protect the rights of individuals. The most important right in the preservation of freedom is one's right to his property, which includes himself. In dreaming of a better society the bishops call for government to make a greater claim on personal freedom. We should reject that nightmare. The great personal freedom Americans have enjoyed has led to unprecedented material and spiritual richness. Before we allow the bishops to foist socialism on America, we should demand they show us where socialism has produced anything close to the human dignity we have.

December 1985

Let's Save the Constitution

WE CELEBRATE the bicentennial of the U.S. Constitution this year. Freedom-loving people all over the world envy the foresight of its Framers. The Constitution (ratified in 1787), and its first ten amendments, the Bill of Rights (ratified in 1791), have preserved our freedoms for nearly 200 years. Two hundred years is a trifle on the scale of human history, but it's eons on the freedom calendar. All of man's history has been one of arbitrary control and abuse by government, and this remains the case in most of the world. Most people have contempt for individual freedom. Lest we become too smug about ourselves, the reason we remain free is not due to some superior genetic strain. We're free mainly because our Founding Fathers gave us some solidly entrenched, difficult to change, rules of the game.

The Constitution was not a perfect recipe for social organization. Its most glaring defects were that it did not extend all of its provisions to blacks and women. These were addressed by the Fourteenth, Fifteenth, and Nineteenth Amendments.

The original Articles of the Constitution tell what the federal government *can* do. It authorizes treaties, collection of taxes, maintenance of armies, and other activities for the general welfare. Men like George Mason and Thomas Jefferson were dissatisfied. They recognized that the history of man was one of governmental abuses and they wanted rules to limit government power: thus our Bill of Rights.

Irrespective of the current debate between Attorney General Ed Meese and the legal establishment over exact interpretation of the Bill of Rights, its intent is clear: to stifle government. It limits government interference with rights to religion, to free speech, to bear arms, to trial by jury, and other freedoms. The Framers did not trust Congress to guard these precious freedoms. On its 200th anniversary, our Constitution is still a powerful document, but it is under siege and threat of despoliation by Congress and the courts. It is undergoing the changes a tyrant would seek, but at a slower pace.

The right of citizens to bear arms, protected by the Second Amendment, faces perennial assault by those who would outlaw possession of guns. That is precisely what a tyrant would want. If you are going to take people's property, the last thing you want them to be is armed. It is probably no coincidence that the Congress's big spenders are also pro gun control.

The Fifth Amendment ends, "[N]or shall private property be taken for public use without just compensation." This provision gives government the power of eminent domain, whereby it can take private property for a *public* use, such as a highway. In *Hawaii Housing Authority* v. *Midkiff* (1984), the U.S. Supreme Court ruled that government could take property from one person and transfer it to another for *private* use. This decision threatens all private property; federal, state, and local governments have only to imagine a public use.

The Constitution's biggest defect is it doesn't spell out what percentage of our earnings Congress can take. It's not clear whether Congress can take some or all of our earnings each April 15th.

We need to remedy the debasement of our Constitution, and the method is provided by Article Five: "The Congress . . . on the application of the Legislatures of two-thirds of the several States, shall call a convention for proposing amendments." Thirty-two state legislatures have already called for convening the constitutional convention; two more are needed.

Wouldn't a convention reestablishing the principles of liberty be a great way to celebrate the Bicentennial?

April 1986

Conservatives vs. Liberals

W HAT'S THE difference between conservatives and liberals? In principle it's hard to find a dime's worth of difference. Many of them are kindred spirits in the sense of wanting to use government force to impose their values on others. They merely differ as to what they wish to forcibly impose on others.

Conservatives are easily identified by their stance on abortion. They argue that abortion is murder and government force should be used to prevent it. They argue that the fetus is a person with the same rights as any other person. What they fail to tell us is what standard of moral conduct says that one person (the fetus) has the right to live off the organs of another when the other person does not wish him to do so.

Liberals, on the other hand, take the position that abortion is a personal choice that should be free from government intervention. They argue that women should be free to do with their bodies as they please. As such, they share my sympathies. But one of their big problems is that they want taxpayers to foot the bill for some abortions. There we part company. In a free society, people should have the right to do with their bodies as they please, but with *their own* money.

Unlike some other Americans, I have not received the divine word from God about abortion. It is a difficult, but personal, decision that I would never want to be placed in a position of deciding. On the other hand, I wouldn't want Congress or the courts to decide for me.

But the liberal stance on personal freedom has a hollow, self-serving ring. It is hypocrisy when they say people should be free to make a momentous decision on whether or not to have an abortion, but not free to choose to work at a wage lower than that specified in the minimum wage law, or not free to say prayers in school.

Conservatives and liberals are kindred spirits as far as government spending is concerned. First, let's make sure we understand what government spending is. Since government has no resources of its own, and since there's no Tooth Fairy handing Congress the funds for the programs it enacts, we are forced to recognize that government spending is no less than the confiscation of one person's property to give it to another to whom it does not belong—in effect, legalized theft.

Liberals believe government should take people's earnings to give to poor people. Conservatives disagree. They think government should confiscate people's earnings and give them to farmers and insolvent banks. The compelling issue to both conservatives and liberals is not whether it is legitimate for government to confiscate one's property to give to another, the debate is over the disposition of the pillage.

Those of us who see Congress as the villain make a serious mistake. We can only blame Congress if we can reasonably expect congressmen to be statesmen with the long-run interests of the United States in mind. That is hardly an adequate description. For the most part, congressmen are merely the brokers in pillage and plunder. They are in office because they promised the voters to use the powers of that office in order for one American to live at the expense of another.

Some might consider this characterization especially harsh. But ask yourself whether a politician could win if he didn't promise to push through highway funds, education grants, and assorted other pork-barrel projects.

All of this means that we, the people, are to blame for the diminution of our freedoms. We can't blame congressmen any more than we can blame pimps for prostitution. Both provide broker services for their customers.

August 1986

Protecting Society

WHEN GOVERNMENTS engage in illegitimate activities, they are bound to fail in those which are legitimate. This is evident in government's failure to protect us from criminals. The Lincoln Institute (1001 Connecticut Ave., N.W., Washington, D.C. 20036), a black think tank headed by Jay Parker, has just documented this failure in *Capital Punishment: An Idea Whose Time Has Come Again* ($3.00).

At 102 murders per 100,000 people, the U.S. murder rate is the highest in the industrialized world. That's more than the death rate in war zones like Northern Ireland, where there are 88 deaths per 100,000. During the Nazi bombing of London, there were 217 deaths per 100,000 people; Detroit has 42.4 murders per 100,000 each year. A baby born today stands a greater chance of being murdered than an American soldier did of being killed in combat during WW II.

Murder was on the decline until we abolished capital punishment. From 1935 to 1940, the murder rate fell from 10,587 to 8,329; this decline continued through two decades with 7,418 murders committed in 1957. Then the late 1960s came along and the death penalty was abandoned. And the murder rate rose from more than 12,000 in 1968, to 18,520 in 1972, to over 22,000 in 1981. While we may debate causes, one conclusion is inescapable: The chances of the execution of murderers has decreased, and the number of murders has risen.

The death penalty has been attacked as cruel and unusual punishment. Nonsense! In 1787, when the Eighth Amendment was being written, the death penalty for murder was in use around the world. Execution often took the form of burning, drawing and quartering, disembowelment, and impalement. Punishment for lesser offenses included: cutting off ears or hands, castration, slitting of the nose, and branding. This kind of punishment, not the execution of murderers, is what the Framers of our Constitution meant by cruel and unusual.

Since the death penalty abolitionists lost their fight on "cruel and unusual" grounds, they have turned their attention to having it abolished on racially discriminatory grounds. Once again, blacks are being used to serve the agenda of other people. Lawyers for the NAACP, Congressional Black Caucus, and the Lawyer's Committee for Civil Rights have asked the Supreme Court to declare Georgia's capital punishment statute unconstitutional. They argue that blacks stand a greater chance of receiving a death sentence for murdering a white than does a white who murders a black. The abolitionists are really reaching in face of the evidence. Twelve blacks are executed per 1,000 arrested for murder while 16 whites are. Only 11 percent of black death-row inmates are executed while 17 percent of whites are.

Abolitionists call for life in prison. *Capital Punishment* reports that murderers sentenced to life in prison are out on the streets in two, seven, or, at worst, 14 years. How would you feel, if a loved one was murdered and you saw the murderer browsing in the shopping mall two years later? The Lincoln Institute booklet cites cases of murderers, with multiple murder convictions, returned to the streets only to murder again.

According to polls, the majority of Americans, including blacks (who comprise more than 50 percent of murder victims), approve of the death penalty. It's about time we make that clear to the politicians and judges.

December 1986

Chapter III

SPENDING, TAXING, AND REGULATING

P<small>EOPLE'S BLIND</small> faith in government's ability to do good is unwarranted. World history provides abundant evidence that government's ability to do bad far outstrips its ability to do good. The reason is rooted in the fact that government has no resources of its own; there is no Santa Claus or Tooth Fairy providing government with resources. If that simple fact is accepted, we are forced to acknowledge that the only way government can give one American a dollar is to take it from another American. Similarly, the only way government can give one American a special advantage is to give some other American a special disadvantage. In slick economic jargon, government allocation of resources is a *zero sum* game (like poker) where the only way one person wins is for another person to lose.

On top of government's limited ability to do good, is government's inability to regulate economic activity. This results because no bureaucrat or set of bureaucrats can ever compile the information that is available through market transactions. No government agency has the ability to coordinate the private plans of millions upon millions of decision-makers making billions upon billions of daily decisions. When people suggest government can regulate economic activity, they implicitly assume it is possible for politicians to successfully substitute their knowledge for the communication, control, and coordination of the market.

Consider the late Leonard Read's query: Can anybody make a pencil? A novice, or a bureaucrat, would quickly answer yes. Just go out and buy the wood, graphite, glue, and rubber. But making a pencil is far more complicated. Let us just peer a wee bit into what is necessary to make a pencil. You need rubber. Rubber comes from Malaysia. Do you know how to raise rubber trees? What pests infect rubber trees? Then consider the fact that the rubber is no good to us in Malaysia; we must somehow get it here. Do you know how to build a ship, make navigation equipment, drill oil or mine coal to provide the ship with fuel, navigate a ship and control the crew? Of course, we also need tools to build the ship, make the navigation equipment, and to mine the oil or coal. In addition, we need food and clothing for the workers. Obviously, this list can go on and on nearly without limit. We can develop a keen appreciation for why there are bottlenecks, shortages, and surpluses in planned economies. We can also understand the Department of Energy's problems when it was regulating oil and gas deliveries in the 1970s, when we found some parts of the country dry and others awash with fuel.

None of this is to say that bureaucrats are incompetent as people. It is to say that economic planning and regulation, with the object of maximizing the material wealth of the nation, is inherently impossible.

The columns that follow discuss some of the effects of spending, taxing, and regulating.

There's a Strong
Case for Gold

THE U.S. Gold Commission, in its report several months back, rejected the restoration of the gold standard and, hence, the prospect for a return to "honest" money. Now there's an excellent book about honest money: *The Case for Gold,* by Representative Ron Paul (R.-Tex.) and Lewis Lehrman (almost governor of New York), published by the Cato Institute, Washington, D.C. *The Case for Gold* is a minority report from the Gold Commission. It was a foregone conclusion at its inception that the commission would recommend against a return to the gold standard.

The reason most politicians, bureaucrats, and interventionists oppose the use of gold as money is that it would make it more difficult for them to "steal" from us. Under fiat money—paper currency—they can steal by simply ordering the Fed to print more dollars. And when you issue more dollars, it lowers the value of those dollars already in circulation. If we had gold-based money, the bureaucrats would have to reach down in the mines for more gold if they wanted increased power. And given the attitude of most bureaucrats, that would be too much like work.

One of the most interesting bits of information in *The Case for Gold* is "the Constitution forbids the states to make anything but gold and silver coin as tender in payment of debt; nor does it permit the federal government to make *anything* a legal tender." Legal tender laws give the federal government the power to force people to accept something in payment of debts even if the people do not want to accept it.

Each Federal Reserve note bears the words, "This note is legal tender for all debts, public and private." The U.S. had no such laws until 1862 when Congress, in violation of the Constitution, enacted them to ensure acceptance of the Lincoln greenbacks, the paper money printed by the Treasury during the Civil War "emergency," which has lasted for 120 years.

But let's get back to government theft. Until 1971, each dollar was 1/35th of an ounce of gold. Now gold sells for over $400 an ounce, which means your dollar is now worth less than 1/400th of an ounce. You figure it out; we've been had. But if gold were the currency, you would have retained your purchasing power.

Lehrman and Rep. Paul give us some fine suggestions for allowing gold and silver to again act as money. First, we must eliminate the capital gains tax on coins. As it stands now, if you trade goods for gold and the nominal price for gold rises, you'd be liable for a capital gains tax. This confiscatory tax must be repealed. We must remove excise and sales taxes that are currently applied to gold and silver transactions.

Any American who wishes to effectively reduce government theft should read *The Case for Gold*. Then demand that your elected representatives vote for, if not the return to a gold standard, at least the elimination of all taxes on coins. That, by the way, would eliminate the effect of "tax" on dollars. And keep in mind that inflation is a tax on dollars.

It boils down to one basic, and irrefutable, fact: *All* gold and silver money is now worth *more* than when it was issued, and all paper currency is now worth *less*.

January 1983

What We Need Is Another Davy Crockett

WITH THE 98th Congress convened, we see many new faces and new agendas. But we wonder whether there is a face and agenda present to match that of Rep. David Crockett, who served Tennessee as a Democrat and later a Whig before moving on to Texas where he fought and died at the Alamo.

One day in the 1800s, the House took up a bill to appropriate money for the widow of a distinguished naval officer. The speaker was about ready to put the bill to a vote when Col. Davy Crockett stood and said, "I have as much respect for the memory of the deceased . . . but we must not permit our respect for the dead or our sympathy for a part of the living to lead us into an act of injustice to the balance of the living."

The frontiersman-turned-lawmaker told the Congress that to forcibly collect tax money from the people to give to others to whom it did not belong was an abuse of its awesome powers. Crockett went on to offer one week of his *own* pay to the widow if every other member of Congress would do the same. The bill failed; and the congressmen didn't offer their *own* money to the widow. To this Crockett observed, "Money with them is nothing but trash when it is to come out of the people. But it is the one great thing for which most of them are striving, and many of them sacrifice honor, integrity, and justice to obtain it." Essentially

Davy Crockett was telling Congress that the money it offered to the widow *was not its to give.*

Government is an unpleasant necessity of civilization. Government is necessary because we must unite to prevent international adversaries and domestic thugs from confiscating our property. And we need government to enforce contracts. These are the legitimate functions of government. But government becomes illegitimate when it does the very things we pay taxes to protect against, such as confiscating our property.

No matter how worthy the cause, it is robbery, theft, and injustice to confiscate the property of one person and give it to another to whom it does not belong. That should be the focal point of debate in Congress. America's totalitarians would have us believe that the issue is "social" versus military spending. In terms of legitimate government that's a false premise. It is legitimate for government to protect us and our property. It is illegitimate for government to, say, confiscate *your* money and give it to me in order for me to buy a television, telephone, or even a hamburger.

This does not mean defense spending is not to be questioned. Military spending is a legitimate government function, but there are corrupt, illegitimate uses to which our military dollars may go: standby jets for officers, private chefs, inefficient contracting resulting in cost overruns, malfunctioning equipment, not to mention all those stockpiled and obsolete items, such as Colt-45 holsters.

Wouldn't it be nice if this Congress, along with the White House, would fight over legitimacy in government? Well they won't—unless you make them. One way to get them started is to reject *your* congressman's promises to get *you* something from government (read: other people's property) and at the same time order him to defend what belongs to you. And while you're at it, tell him, if he sees a worthy cause, to reach down in his *own* pocket, to fund it, because what belongs to you is not his to give away.

January 1983

A Skeptic's Challenge

SOCIAL SECURITY is at once a bad deal, a lie, and a national obstruction. To many Americans, this statement falls just short of attacking God, country, and motherhood, so let me explain.

A study by Peter J. Ferrara, commissioned by the Washington-based Cato Institute, reports that a worker who enters the work force in 1980, earns an average salary all his life, and then retires at age 65, would receive social security payments of $15,000 a year in constant 1980 dollars for him and his spouse. Had the worker instead put the same amount of money he paid as social security taxes into a private fund yielding a real return of 6 percent, the couple could not only retire on an annual income of $28,000 but also, when they died, leave a $500,000 estate to their children. If they didn't want to leave a bequest, the couple could enjoy an annual income of $45,000 until death.

An officially contrived misconception about social security is that the employer pays half the payroll tax. The truth of the matter is that both the employer share and the employee share come out of the *employee's* paycheck. The employer treats "his" share just as he treats any other fringe benefit. The employee's cash pay is adjusted downward to reflect the noncash pay. There are more lies. You're told that social security payments are contributions. A contribution is *voluntary*. Social security *taxes* are not. You're told that these "contributions" go into a trust fund for future payments. No such thing. Your only guarantee of future payments is the willingness of workers to pay increasing taxes. The maximum tax now is $4,342 a year and will probably be $10,000 by 1990.

If a person were able to invest the money now taken by social security taxes in a private retirement plan, that money would be available to investors for the purchase of plant and equipment. But no such thing happens with social security payments, totaling $180 billion last year, because as soon as you pay social security taxes, they immediately go to a social security recipient. Martin Feldstein, chairman of the President's Council of Economic Advisers, has estimated that social security reduces private savings by about 35 percent. Feldstein concludes that because of reduced savings—and hence investment—our GNP is lower than it would otherwise be.

Despite conventional wisdom and political demagoguery, the social security mess is not so much a problem for older people as it is for younger people. They are the ones who will pay increasingly higher taxes and find, in the autumn of their lives, a bankrupted, politically unacceptable system. Recent surveys demonstrate pessimism among our young. A 1982 Washington Post-ABC News poll found that 66 percent of those under 45 and 74 percent of those under 30 believe that social security won't be in existence when they retire. A 1981 New York Times-CBS News poll found that 75 percent between ages 25 and 34 doubted that they would receive the social security benefits they have been promised. The same poll found that 73 percent of all Americans had lost confidence in social security.

Nobody with the slightest bit of compassion suggests turning old people out into the streets. Our first order of business is to recognize that social security, while well intentioned, was a mistake—a mistake that won't be corrected by raising social security taxes, raising retirement age, reducing benefits, or dragging federal employees and congressmen into the morass. These steps just postpone the crisis for three or four years, the time between elections. The solution is to make social security private, because *every* estimate shows that a private retirement program, such as a mandatory IRA, would be superior.

How do we get from here to there? First we acknowledge that among current workers those above a certain age have already paid so much into social security that they would do better staying in the system than abandoning it. That age is approximately 40. Everyone who is younger than that would leave the social-security system and kiss goodbye the money already contributed. The sweetener is that at 65 they will be as well off and most likely better off than they would have been with social security. Those people over 40 who desire to stay in social security would continue making payments and would receive benefits when they retire. All who are already retired would get the benefits now pre-scribed. There would be a shortfall of revenues against expenditures—perhaps more than $100 billion—that would have to be funded out of general revenues. While it is a frightening figure, we can count on it to fall rapidly.

Privatizing social security will make the nation better off economi-cally by putting billions of dollars into our capital-starved economy. It will avoid social problems as well. For if we continue with the present system, a day will come when young people, paying 30 percent of their wages in social security taxes to support some old people, will begin to get other ideas about what to do with old people. That's an increasing concern of mine as the years go by.

January 1983

Hunger Just a Hoax Played on the Public

Hunger in America is the latest hoax being played on a vulnerable American public—vulnerable because of its generosity.

Presidential Counselor Ed Meese was right in pointing out that hunger was not a significant problem in our country and suggested that the widely publicized soup kitchen traffic was not so much a result of hunger as a manifestation of man's tireless quest for a free lunch.

I agree with Meese, for I've seen no people dying from starvation à la Chad, Bangladesh, or Ethiopia. I rather suspect most people seen in U.S. soup kitchen lines have a few coins in their jeans they'd rather keep for items not handed out free—like wine, dope, or cigarettes.

There is malnutrition in America. Several studies report even middle class households suffer from malnutrition. But most of the malnutrition in America stems from ignorance of what constitutes a nutritious diet, rather than inadequate funds to purchase such a diet.

Even *if* there were some residual hunger in America, it's not the fault of taxpayers, who have forked over $22 billion in 1983 for food stamps and other nutrition programs, which do not include this summer's big cheese giveaway. Nor does it include all subsidized school lunches that go to middle and upper income families.

Reduced to its common denominator, the hunger charade is just another attack on President Reagan over the "fairness" issue. The people who use this issue neither care about nor have the slightest notion of fairness.

Remember, government has no resources of its own. The *only* way government can give one American a dollar is to first confiscate that dollar from another American. (If you think confiscate is too strong a word, try telling the IRS you won't give up your money.)

What's fair about this? To put the fairness issue in another perspective, ask: If I enjoy the use of a car, a coat, or a hamburger, in terms of fairness, *who* should be made to pay for it?

None of this should suggest a callous disregard for America's unfortunate. It does suggest that the hundreds of billions of dollars we've thrown at the problem has not only been immoral but ineffective in eliminating a debilitating dependency for many Americans.

December 1983

Farm Handouts Expose
Congressional Hypocrites

CONSERVATIVES DISAGREE about lots of things. But if they seek instant agreement, they talk about handouts. Conservatives love to rail against handouts—like Aid to Families with Dependent Children, food stamps, and public housing.

Some conservatives, however, are selective in their railing against handouts. They are *against* handouts to the poor and *for* those to the nonpoor, and in this case they don't have a moral leg to stand on and deserve contempt from people of goodwill.

At the risk of re-offending readers who say, "I agree with you about everything else, but disagree with you about farm programs," let's talk about an article in the April *Reader's Digest*, "Fiasco on the Farm." Author James Bovard shares a few disgusting findings: National Farms is a huge agribusiness operating in Nebraska, Texas, and Arkansas. In 1983 it received a $35 million federal corn and wheat handout. Belridge Farms, a Shell Oil subsidiary, received a $2 million federal handout linked to these same commodities. California's South Lake Farms was visited by folks from the U.S. Department of Agriculture (USDA). When Santa Claus' helpers left, South Lake Farms was richer by $24 million worth of federal cotton. The USDA is an equal opportunity

Santa Claus giving handouts to hundreds of thousands of other farmers.

You can bet Santa didn't get the goodies from some elves in the North Pole. Get your W-2 form and take a look in the mirror; you're the elf. These goodies are a part of Payment in Kind (PIK) where farmers were given $10 billion of government-owned (meaning taxpayer-financed) farm surplus in return for giving their promise to leave 48 million acres idle—in total, the size of Nebraska.

PIK is an insane program. It makes sense to people like Senator Bob Dole (R.-Kan.), who is wooing farm votes. First, it idled much of the world's best farm land in a year when millions were starving in other countries. Second, hundreds of farm equipment and supply shops closed down because farmers weren't planting crops and didn't need as many supplies. An estimated quarter-of-a-million jobs were lost among suppliers and farm canning, milling, and transportation workers. And for good measure, the PIK program will add $20 to $30 billion to America's 1984 food bill.

But the PIK program is not the only farm handout; it's just the latest. When Carter left office, farm subsidies totalled $3 billion. With the fiscally "conservative" Reagan administration in office, farm handouts are a whopping $19 billion with PIK added on top of that.

Honey farmers get some $33 million of your money. Then there's the $1.5 billion crop disaster program which encourages farmers to grow crops in high-risk areas. If the crop is destroyed, the government (read: you) pays them. That's something. PIK pays farmers *not* to grow crops on good land; the farm disaster program pays farmers to grow crops on bad land. The Congressional Budget Office (CBO) has found that crop disaster payments go mostly to a small number of farmers who yearly plant crops on high-risk land.

There are many farm handouts; but let's call them what they *really* are: a form of legalized theft. Essentially, a congressman tells his farm constituency, "Vote for me. I'll use my office to take another American's money and give it to you." Now, the congressman doesn't phrase it just that way, but the end result is the same. These handouts have been so successful in getting votes that Senator Dole is designing a plan to give farmers their 1985 handout before the 1984 elections.

But let's change focus a bit. Remember the hunger flap where congressmen got on their high horses to weep about hunger in America? How can one say on television he cares about hunger while in the privacy of his office, egged on by lobbyists and other hustlers, he votes for measures to raise food prices? Such a person is an unprincipled, hypocritical scoundrel.

If any congressmen wishes to debate or sue this writer for what is in this column, then like my friend Bill Simon, who told them what they were (*The Wall Street Journal,* February 9, 1984), I welcome the opportunity. And I *will* win.

March 1984

The Costs of Political Benefits

B USINESSMEN KNOW correct decisions require accurate information. The decision on how to produce and distribute a given product requires at least a good guess about the pluses and minuses involved. That's just plain good business sense.

Americans should know the costs and benefits of government programs so, like businessmen, we too can make good decisions. Like any other decision-makers, we Americans, through our representatives, need to ask, "What does the program cost?" and "Is there a cheaper way to get the benefit?"

Take the Reagan decision to aid Harley-Davidson by slapping a 49 percent tariff on imported Japanese motorcycles. We can debate whether Americans should save Harley-Davidson—what if we went to war and couldn't get needed motorcycles from the Japanese?—but like any decision, prudence requires that we ask, "What does it cost? Is there a cheaper way to do it?" But with tariffs and quotas that question is hardly ever asked and debated.

Had I been involved in the Harley-Davidson decision, I would have asked the company, "How much money do you need to survive to compete with the Japanese, whom we utterly defeated in World War II?" Harley's officers might have said they need $200 million. Then that would have been the question put to Americans: "All those in favor of $200 million in aid to dependent motorcycle producers, answer by saying 'aye.' "

There are at least three good reasons why my proposal is better than tariffs. First, because of what economists call "deadweight loss." To get Harley-Davidson $200 million, it might cost American consumers and Japanese producers $300 million. Second, competition always reveals superior production techniques. Third, if you are going to do something, it is always a good idea to know what it costs. As the French philosopher Frederic Bastiat said about tariffs, they are "negative railways" that serve to increase costs rather than lower them. For consistency, supporters of tariffs should also advocate returning to stagecoaches for transportation.

One does not have to ponder long to figure out that my modest proposal would fall on deaf ears in the halls of Congress, the White House, and offices of lobbyists. Tariffs provide for a comfy relationship between businessmen and politicians. Congressmen don't have the fortitude to vote for tax increases. They prefer hidden taxes like inflation and deficits; that's why they are trying to repeal tax indexing.

Like inflation, tariffs are a great means to pass out favors in order to get votes and political contributions. You make a handout without the unpleasantness of voting for a tax increase. Recipients of tariff protection like it because it makes their handouts easier to get and less obvious. Workers in the companies involved like it because it enables their wages to exceed their productivity. Hidden taxes, such as tariffs, make everybody's job a bit easier. After all, who could expect an "Aid to Dependent Motorcycle Companies" bill for $500 million to pass Congress without some congressmen losing their jobs?

Now, notice that my modest proposal does not even attempt to debate the often stated benefits of tariffs, such as the strategic necessity of having motorcycles, cheese, sugar, etc., in the event of war. It is simply an attempt to determine the costs of political choices so the American people can intelligently choose among them.

April 1984

Producing Poor Children

THE GRAMM-RUDMAN-HOLLINGS Act calls for federal spending reductions. Soon we're going to see a long overdue spending fight in Congress as various lawmakers attempt to protect favorite programs from the budget axe. Forces of "evil" will line up to protect military expenditures while forces of "good" will rally to prevent budget balancing on the "backs of the poor."

Those who are truly concerned about the poor should consider the increasing evidence that the worst thing for the poor is government handouts. Charles Murray's book, *Losing Ground*, documents that fact. Now economics Professors Lowell Gallaway and Richard Vedder, at the Athens campus of Ohio University, provide more evidence in two papers, "The 'New' Structural Poverty," and, "Suffer the Little Children."

In 1983, the official poverty rate was 15.3 percent. This was greater than the 1966 poverty rate, which stood at 14.7 percent. By 1984, the rate had fallen to 14.4 percent—not much different from what it was in 1966. After billions upon billions were spent in the War on Poverty, the best we can claim is that poverty has remained unchanged. Where did we go wrong? According to Gallaway and Vedder, as well as many other observers, the answer is simple. We forgot that poor people are poor, but they're not stupid. Poor people respond to economic incentives just like the rest of us.

Between 1970 and 1983, the national poverty rate among children rose from 14.9 to 21.7 percent. Gallaway and Vedder find remarkable differences when the statistics are broken down by state. In New Jersey between 1969 and 1979, poverty among children rose by 53.2 percent, while in Wyoming it *fell* by 34.7 percent.

Why should this rate vary from state to state? Gallaway and Vedder say part of the answer is due to differences in income growth, but welfare benefits paid to parents also play a role. West Virginia in 1969 had a poverty rate among children of 24.3 percent, and in New York it was 12.7 percent. By 1979, the West Virginia rate had dropped to 18.5 percent, while New York's had risen to 19 percent. New York's Aid to Families with Dependent Children (AFDC) was 90 percent higher than West Virginia's.

Gallaway and Vedder conclude that if you set out to devise a system to create poverty among children, you couldn't do much better than the present welfare system. Poor children come from poor parents. To the extent that parents make choices that make them poor, their children will be poor. Several income maintenance experiments (particularly those in Seattle and Denver) show that welfare reduces work incentives. Gallaway and Vedder show that welfare payments, above some threshold amount, lead to higher poverty rates. People simply choose the tax-free subsidy to a low-wage job that might lead to a higher future income.

Welfare has had devastating effects on the black family. In 1960, 20 percent of black children lived in father-absent households; today it's nearly 60 percent. Now their father is Uncle Sam! White liberals called for it. Back in December 1964, Tom Wicker, writing in *The New York Times,* said ". . . a decent living ought to be made available not just to an eligible few but to everyone, and without degrading restrictions and police-like investigations."

Throughout our history, rapid economic growth has been the most effective anti-poverty weapon. Today, government programs have made many poor Americans immune to economic growth. That's the new structural poverty—and it's mean.

February 1986

Does It Matter Who Controls Congress?

ONCE AGAIN the Democrats control both Houses of Congress. But what's the *real* significance of these changes resulting from the 1986 elections? For the most part, little or nothing, because a politician is a politician. Let's look at the record.

When the Republicans swept the White House and the Senate in 1980, the budget deficit was just under $60 billion; the national debt was $1 trillion. Here in 1986, as the Republicans lost the Senate, the budget deficit was well over $200 billion; the national debt nearly $2 trillion. Had the Democrats been in control of the White House and Senate, could our fiscal condition have been worse? The Republicans' major contribution has been to lend "respectability" to fiscal cowardice and irresponsibility.

No matter who won control in the elections, the congressional agenda for 1987–88 still would be the same—raise taxes. Congressmen will say, "We've got to do something about the deficit," but if tax increases could balance the budget, it would have been done a long time ago. Look at the record. In 24 of the last 25 years, the federal budget has been in the red. And in 22 of those years, there has been some kind of tax increase. The problem is not taxes; it's spending. It's that simple.

What about the tax reform law? It has some good features, namely reducing individual marginal tax rates and cutting out or reducing some tax favors. Its bad features are the increased business tax and its anti-savings and anti-investment features. But tax favors (loopholes) are bound to return. Here's the scoop: Prior to this year's tax changes, Congress had little to trade in the way of tax favors for votes; there were too many loopholes. Tax reform closed many of the loopholes. Now they can be resold for votes. Therein lies the agenda for the 100th Congress of the United States—selling loopholes.

Another item on the agenda for the incoming Congress is Aid to Dependent Farmers. Election results showed Congress did not give enough of our earnings to farmers. But a Republican-controlled White House and Senate was far more generous than Jimmy Carter and the Democrats had been of late. When Carter left office, Aid to Dependent Farmers (agricultural subsidies) stood at $5 billion. This year's handouts topped $30 billion, still the farmers wanted more.

In some ways, the Republicans deserved to lose. Instead of becoming statesmen, it was business as usual—tinkering here and tinkering there. But as I have often said, it takes a strong politician to buck the will of his constituency and take the moral high ground. We expect that of South African Prime Minister P.W. Botha, but not U.S. politicians.

Republicans had several "windows of opportunity" to be statesmen, but they had the spines of jellyfish. They could have thrown their weight behind a constitutional amendment to set a definite limit on how much money government can take from the taxpayers. They had the political power to drastically cut off welfare programs, including those to businessmen, unions, senior citizens, and farmers. Instead, the Republicans proved that it's just a matter of whose ox is being gored.

There's only one solution to our fiscal mess and bloated government. We must get two state legislatures to call for reconvening the Constitutional Convention for the limited purposes of passing a balanced-budget/spending-limitation amendment; 32 states have already done so. Congress has proved that it can't be trusted to guard our rights to our earnings anymore than the Framers trusted them to guard our rights to freedom of religion and speech. How much religious freedom and free speech do you think we would have now were they not constitutionally guarded rights?

November 1986

Getting Serious About Welfare

THE CHRISTMAS season not only ushers in brightly decorated shopping malls, gleeful children, and family gatherings, it also reminds us of the poor. That part of Christmas is heard in the ringing bells of the Salvation Army volunteers and food and toy donation drives throughout the nation. This is a splendid testament to our Judeo-Christian ethic. But while charity might be man's greatest virtue, it is no cure for poverty.

Poor people face many handicaps, but the most serious is their treatment as charity cases. It wasn't always this way. In times past, if a husband died, or became incapacitated, or abandoned his family, his wife and family got temporary relief to help them through the tough times—but they were expected to get on their feet and off relief as soon as possible. All that has changed today. People actually choose welfare as a permanent way of life because it is their "right."

Without a doubt, people do get in trouble and need assistance. As generous Americans, we rush to help, but we do it in a thoughtless way, forgetting to ask: How does our help affect a person's incentive to help himself? Anyone who has raised children knows that is a hard question to answer. Any loving parent knows there is always the temptation to bail our children out "just one more time." But how well does dependency-creating love serve the child's long-run interests?

Aren't we careless when we ignore that question in our dealings with poor people? We just bail them out year after year and generation after generation, never asking what we are doing to incentives. How truly compassionate is it to have a system which encourages dependency and discourages people from achieving their potential?

Consider education. What motivates a youngster to learn and behave in school? It is the parentally instilled realization that he needs an education to support himself. But with our current welfare system, all that is distorted; instead of making the sacrifices necessary for a good education, some people put their creative energy into tapping sources of public support.

What motivates a person to take a low-paying, entry-level job? It used to be there were no other alternatives. Now there is welfare. But by taking a low-paying, entry-level job, a person was not only learning work habits, getting some skills, and learning about other opportunities, he was establishing himself as a reliable worker and gaining the dignity of supporting himself.

Even among my many liberal friends who disagree with me on many issues, I know of none who would treat their children as we treat poor people. They would not provide incentives for their fourteen-year-old daughters to have babies. They stress to their children the importance of education. They often see to it their children live with the unpleasant consequences of their behavior. Do they show the same compassion and common sense toward the poor? No, they take the position that the poor have a *right* to dependency.

I am not proposing we eliminate welfare tomorrow. It would be cruel to go cold-turkey on people we have addicted to welfare. We need to start a withdrawal program. A first step is to make welfare eligibility temporary and its conditions as onerous as possible. But most of all we need to get serious and examine whether we are really best serving the poor and ourselves with the current dependency-creating welfare programs.

December 1986

Chapter IV

EDUCATION AND LABOR

THE PRESIDENT'S National Commission on Excellence in Education concluded we are a nation at risk. An alarming number of youngsters are illiterate and innumerate despite the billions of federal, state, and local dollars poured into education. This might be the first generation of Americans that is less well educated than its parents.

Poor education easily translates into employment problems, especially when jobs are demanding increasing technological expertise. Black Americans, who receive the poorest education, encounter the highest unemployment rates. Civil rights organizations, government task forces, and politicians ask: What can government do to ameliorate problems of poor education and unemployment? No one gives consideration to the idea that government can help best by reducing its role in regulating education and labor markets.

As a group, blacks receive grossly inferior education, but there are notable exceptions, mostly in *non*-government schools. Los Angeles' Marcus Garvey School's black elementary school students achieve higher scores than their white counterparts. Students at Marva Collins' Westside Preparatory School exceed the achievement of their Chicago government school counterparts by a wide margin. Eighty percent of Philadelphia's Ivy Leaf School students score at or above the national norm on standardized tests and some even score, two, three, and four years above.

For the most part, these independent black school students come from low- and middle-income backgrounds. Why have these schools achieved what has proved to be elusive, if not impossible, at government schools? There might be many answers but there are several stark differences between non-government and government schools. In the government schools, teachers get paid whether or not students can read and write; principals get paid whether or not students can read and write; students receive diplomas whether or not they can read and write; and finally, it is nearly impossible for the school to fire incompetent teachers or expel kids who are troublemakers. Non-government schools do not have the same constraints.

No one can say that higher budgets account for the relative success of the non-government schools. Typically, they operate on budgets that are tiny fractions, often not even a third, of government schools.

To improve black education, we should enhance the opportunity for students to leave schools doing a poor job, at a high cost, and enter schools doing a good job at a lower cost. The policy tool to promote this objective is an educational voucher system designed along the lines of the G.I. Bill.

After youngsters are deprived of a good education, they are expected to compete in labor markets with significant government-mandated handicaps. The minimum wage law is one such handicap. The maze of labor regulations is another. While government restrictions have their greatest effects on blacks, we should not be blind to the fact that they handicap anybody who can be described as low-skilled or less-preferred.

The columns in this section examine the problems created by government control and interference in education and labor.

I Done Told You

THE CAT'S finally out of the bag. For years this writer has shared the view of Thomas Sowell that students—particularly black students—have been receiving what amounts to a fraudulent education: The fraud being that the education establishment warrants, by issuing a diploma, that black high school graduates can read, write, and compute at a twelfth grade level; the fact of the matter is that the greater percentage cannot even perform at the eighth grade level. This is nothing less than a cruel lie and an unconscionable fraud.

That's my conclusion, but a National Commission on Excellence in Education (NCEE) report provides the evidence. Part of the NCEE findings are that 13 percent of all seventeen-year-olds are functionally illiterate and 40 percent of minority youth are functionally illiterate. Average achievement of all high schools is down. Standardized test scores steadily declined from 1963 to 1980. Only one-fifth of the nation's high school seniors can write a persuasive essay, and only one-third of them can solve mathematical problems requiring more than a couple of steps.

One of the most depressing aspects of this morass is the recent revelation that many teachers, disproportionately black, have not *themselves* mastered basic reading, writing, and computational skills. Quite often in ghetto schools it boils down to the blind leading the blind. In Tallahassee, Florida, prospective teachers must take a test. In the most recent test, the passing percentage among blacks was 35 percent, compared to 90 percent for whites. Black leaders label competency tests culturally biased. I'd like to know how. For example one question asks for the sum of $3 + 905 + 66 + 821$. How is that biased?

Besides destroying the lifetime chances of millions of black kids, fraudulent education aggravates another problem. For nearly two decades we've had laws prohibiting racial discrimination in employment and college admissions. Civil rights activists and black "spokesmen" find that this nondiscriminatory policy is not enough. Thus, they push for racial quotas in employment and college admissions.

How can anyone tell whether a company engages in discriminatory hiring and promotion policy when blacks are so grossly ill-prepared. If the Los Angeles Lakers had no black basketball players on the team I'd know for a fact they had a racially discriminatory hiring policy; I'd stake my life on it. But if there are no black physicists at the Lawrence Radiation Laboratories you can't be as sure.

And it all boils down to the poor quality of black education. If the Grand Dragon of the Ku Klux Klan wanted to deny blacks upward mobility, reinforce racial stereotypes of black mental incompetence, and foster racial conflict, he couldn't find a better tool than our public education system.

But the solution? We must enhance parental choice and power. Middle-class and rich parents who come up against low-quality education can simply move to a neighborhood with better public schools. But considering the price of suburban homes, $100,000 or more, poor parents don't have that choice. There are some poor black parents who are managing to scrape together a few dollars to take the next best alternative. They send their children to parochial schools, community schools, or Black Muslim schools. According to several studies, including the recent Coleman Report, these non-public schools are doing a superior job. More poor parents could choose this alternative if we had a voucher system or a tuition tax credit program. Needless to say, the public education establishment wants none of this; it gives parents effective power to reject educational fraud. You'd think that since blacks suffer most from rotten education, that the NAACP, Urban League, and black lawmakers would be for vouchers or tuition tax credits. Wrong. Black civil rights groups represent the interests of middle-class blacks, a large percentage of whom are public school teachers who, like their white counterparts, are not interested in accountability either.

That's life in the big city. But I shall be eternally grateful that I received virtually all my education before it became fashionable for whites to "like" black people.

May 1983

All It Takes Is Guts

W<small>HY CAN'T</small> our youngsters read, write, and compute? Why will this be the first generation of Americans more poorly educated than its parents? If you ask Albert Shanker, president of the American Federation of Teachers (AFT), the answer is, "Teacher salaries are too low." Ask a liberal you'll get, "It's racism exacerbated by the Reagan administration."

Violence in schools is a good part of our problem. According to a *Philadelphia Inquirer* story, "Schools Search for a Way to Stop Violence" (11/14/83), there were 2,449 "serious incidents" reported by Philadelphia school principals in 1982. If you think a "serious incident" means breaking a window or cursing at a teacher, think again. "Incidents" in Philadelphia schools included 294 assaults on teachers, 449 assaults against students, and 348 cases of weapons possession in school. Assaults not only include battery, holdup, and rape, they also include knifing, shooting, and murder. Several weeks ago, Do Manh, a Vietnamese student, was beaten into unconsciousness, sustaining a broken neck, by two black students at University City High School, a "magnet" school (all the magnetism in the world would not draw my kid there). The kids arrested for the attack are now back in school. In fact, it's been years since the school system expelled a kid.

The tragic thing is that *reported* incidents seriously understate victimization. Many teachers and students don't report holdups, rapes, and property destruction not only for fear of reprisal but of losing their jobs as well. Principals underreport for fear of being judged ineffective by superiors.

Now guess what the Philadelphia Board of Education wants to do? You've got it. They want to fund a *study* to see what can be done.

America's Future, published in New Rochelle, New York, describes one man who doesn't need studies or reports. When Joseph Clark was assigned as principal to Eastside High School in Paterson, New Jersey, he found: teacher assaults, students carrying guns, drugs being bought and sold on campus, and sexual intercourse in the school's corridors and bathrooms.

All that's been changed. At Eastside, where enrollment is two-thirds black, one-third Hispanic, in the space of one year 82 percent of ninth graders passed a basic math test compared with 55 percent the previous year. Fifty-six percent passed an English skills test compared to 39 percent the preceding year.

What complex program did Joseph Clark use to bring about a learning environment at Eastside? It's easy. Mr. Clark during his *first* week as principal expelled 300 of the school's 3,000 students. The word spread like wildfire that anyone that even looked crosseyed would answer to Principal Clark. Back in my day we called that kicking a certain part of the anatomy.

Eastside used to have an eighteen-man security force in its hallways. It now has four guards *outside* the school—to prevent troublemakers from entering. Teachers can assign homework, teach, and counsel students, instead of trying to defend themselves. Eastside has been declared a *model* school by New Jersey's governor. Dr. Frank Napier, Paterson's superintendent of schools, praising Eastside summed it up well, "Principal Clark may be unorthodox in his approach but it's hard to argue with success." I don't call Clark unorthodox; just old-fashioned. The do-gooders can keep their studies; I'll take Mr. Joseph Clark.

November 1983

Children Need
Do-It-Yourself Options

PUBLIC EDUCATION is in shambles—particularly that delivered to blacks. Meaningful measures to improve education, such as education vouchers or tuition tax credits, are roundly denounced as racist, elitist, and anti-education by the education establishment and its patrons. They reason that poor blacks would be hurt by anything that threatens the established education monopoly.

The National Center for Neighborhood Enterprise (NCNE), headquartered in Washington, D.C., and directed by Robert Woodson, is engaged in work that reveals the self-serving arguments of the education establishment.

The NCNE has identified more than 250 independent black, Hispanic, American Indian, and Asian schools. Most are located in inner-city, low-income neighborhoods. Enrollment ranges from 22 to 800 students. They have an open-door policy and require in-house or standardized testing for placement. The term of student enrollment ranges from two to seven years. Graduates go on to other private schools or specialized and selective public high schools. Most of the neighborhood schools receive the bulk of their income from tuitions, which range from $800 to $2,000 a year. Additional income is derived from foundations, churches, community organizations, and parental fundraising activities.

The drive and ambition of poor parents to protect their children from destruction by public schools has produced notable successes. Last

October, Tony Brown reported in *Washington Afro-American* that Los Angeles' Marcus Garvey Elementary School's black pre-schoolers could spell all the days of the week and months of the year, *and* add, subtract, and divide. That's remarkable considering the fact that, according to the April 27, 1984, *Washington Post,* a student-teacher in a Virginia classroom couldn't spell November. Among the other notable independent black schools are Mrs. Wallie Simpson's Lower East Side Community School in New York, Father George Clements' Holy Angels School, and Marva Collins' Westside Preparatory, both in Chicago.

Contrary to claims by the education establishment and its dupes among black "leaders," students who attend these schools are neither rich nor middle-class in most cases. They are children of working parents, some of whom work two jobs in order to pay the tuition. Some do miscellaneous jobs at the school to pay their children's tuition.

The thousands of black children who attend independent community schools are being spared the damage being done by the public schools. But instead of more success which would be assured by vouchers or tuition tax credits, black civil rights groups and black politicians acting on the economic interests of the educational establishment are saying no. In justifying his position against tuition tax credits, presidential aspirant Jesse Jackson says, "We shouldn't destroy public schools." That's great, but Jackson's son attends St. Albans, Washington's most elite private school, not some public school in Chicago's slums. If you'd question Jesse about this he'd probably say, "My son can't wait for public schools to become great."

Education vouchers or tuition tax credits are essentially like a G.I. Bill extended to primary and secondary schools. Parents would have effective choice and control over their children's education. While all parents would benefit, the chief beneficiaries would be those held captive by the education establishment. Well-to-do, inner-city parents, like Jackson and D.C. delegate Walter Fauntroy, can send their children to elite private schools. But to give more poor parents comparable ability to opt out we need enabling tools, such as vouchers or tuition tax credits.

Robert Woodson's NCNE report on black independent schools proves poor people can, given a chance, provide their own solutions to their own education problems. They've gone a long way without the help of, and despite, the education establishment.

June 1984

What of Miss Liberty's Motto?

HAVING WEATHERED years in New York harbor, the Statue of Liberty is being restored in anticipation of its centennial celebration in 1986. Miss Liberty, France's gift to us to commemorate U.S.-French friendship dating back to the Revolutionary War, has been a welcome sight to tens-of-millions of immigrants seeking freedom, hope, and prosperity.

The weather's toll on the grand Lady pales in comparison to the erosion of her spirit which is captured by the inscription: "Give me your tired, your poor, your huddled masses yearning to breathe free, the wretched refuse of your teeming shore. Send these, the homeless, tempest-tost, to me. I lift my lamp beside the golden door."

That expression of man's humanity to man was seriously diminished during the recent political debate leading to Congress' approval of the new immigration law—the Simpson-Mazzoli Act. Among its features are amnesty for Mexican illegals who've resided here since before 1982; citizenship for Mexicans if they keep a clean record and learn English and civics; and heavy penalties for employers who hire illegal aliens.

House passage of the controversial bill was by a narrow five vote margin. There was considerable opposition to its amnesty feature. According to *The Washington Post*, Rep. Kent R. Hance (D.-Tex.) said,

"You're missing the entire issue—the issue in this debate is jobs. If it's one job [taken by a legalized alien], it's one too many." Rep. Clay Shaw (R.-Fla.) asked, "How many people can the United States accommodate and the quality of life continue?. . . We must put the citizens who are here to work first."

Rep. Peter Rodino (D.-N.J.) got it right when he said illegal immigrants are a decent society composed of people who came here seeking an opportunity. Work and opportunity lie at the heart of the issue. Unions and their followers want to close our borders. None of this is new, just the language and tactics have changed.

Compare the rhetoric of today's restrictionists with that of the founder of the American Federation of Labor, Samuel Gompers, "But the Caucasians are not going to let their standard of living be destroyed by Negroes, Chinamen, Japs, or any others." (*Federationist, 9/19/05*). Gompers elaborated on this in U.S. Senate Document 137 (1902): "Some Reasons For Chinese Exclusion, Meat Vs. Rice: American Manhood Against Asiatic Coolieism, Which Shall Survive" where he said, "The yellow man found it natural to lie, cheat and murder and ninety-nine out of one-hundred Chinese are gamblers. . . . [H]e goes joyfully back [from work] to his slum and his burrow to the grateful luxury of his normal surroundings—vice, filth, and an atmosphere of horror."

Immigration has always been good for America. It was good in the case of the Irish, the Italians, the Jews, the Poles, and all other nationalities; and it is still good today with Mexicans joining our ethnic mix. When yesterday's immigrants migrated here we did not have a welfare state, and therefore we knew people would work when they got here; the alternative was starvation. Today, because of the welfare state, we cannot be so sure. People can come, not work, and live off the rest of us. We have too many American *citizens* doing that now; we don't need more. We *do* need people who will work.

Mexico will have to get its own house in order. We need to reduce the welfare state and continue those policies that contribute to a rapidly growing economy. But meanwhile, what do we do with the inscription on the base of Miss Liberty?

July 1984

Hens, Ants, Grasshoppers, and Pigs

O̲UR UNDERSTANDING of things like the Second Law of Thermodynamics, savings and investment, and hygiene is very important. But these can be awesomely complicated subjects. To make them less complicated, people adopt rules-of-thumb, formulate adages, and create nursery rhymes. For instance, the Second Law of Thermodynamics is captured in "Humpty-Dumpty"—no process is reversible. The importance of savings and investment are underscored in "The Little Red Hen," and "The Ant and the Grasshopper." Hygiene is taught by the adage, "Cleanliness is next to Godliness." All this is cross-cultural in the sense that there's a Humpty-Dumpty- and Little Red Hen-type story in virtually every culture.

As a result of modern education, we've forsaken tales like "The Little Red Hen" and "The Ant and the Grasshopper." We can see the results of this neglect in today's demagogic rhetoric that disparages the well-to-do and the rich and darn near deifies the slovenly, the misfits, and the bums. Nobody who has read "The Little Red Hen" could feel sorry for the lazy slovenly barnyard animals who had no bread. After all, they rejected the Red Hen's repeated job offers.

Similarly, who could feel sorry for the hungry Grasshopper who fiddled away the summer while the Ant slaved to gather food? Furthermore, nobody who saw the Red Hen eating bread while the other barnyard animals had none, or saw the Grasshopper starving during the winter while the Ant dined would say, "That Red Hen and Ant are *lucky.*" They'd probably say the slovenly barnyard animals and Grasshopper are getting their just desserts. Who would argue that social justice could be best served by forcibly taking the Hen's or the Ant's property and *redistributing* it to the other barnyard animals or the Grasshopper?

When it comes to real life, seldom do we "read" the whole story. People see a rich corporation like IBM and wonder, "Why should its owners have all the money when I don't; it's not fair." But they didn't see its founders mortgaging their homes to create electronic equipment, slaving in their garages to the wee hours, and taking big risks.

People read the success story of Levi Strauss with all the resulting riches and say it's not fair. But they ignore the beginning of the story where the man worked long days as a traveling peddler, striking hard bargains with wholesalers, and saving every nickel rather than partying once in a while.

Wealth in this world is seldom a result of pure luck. Virtually all of it comes from successful individual efforts to please one's fellow man; this is particularly true in the case of the capitalistic economies. Levi Strauss or IBM cannot force people to buy jeans or data processing equipment and systems. That means if they want wealth they must please people.

In fact, that's what competition is all about: "outpleasing" your competitors to win over the consumers. Sears tries to outplease Montgomery Ward; General Motors tries to outplease Ford; Apple tries to outplease IBM. The penalty for pleasing insufficiently is going out of business (except when government interferes, as in the Chrysler bailout). Notice how Amtrak and the U.S. Postal Service were not under a lot of pressure to please until they started facing private-sector competition. The reason is that unlike Levi Strauss and IBM, they have the power, through the IRS, to take our money—using our taxes to compete with private, taxpaying firms.

Let's return the tales of "The Little Red Hen" and "The Ant and the Grasshopper" to the curriculum, so we can channel our anger towards the right people.

July 1984

Beware of the 'Experts'

THOSE 45 or over probably remember elementary school drills where we had to write continuous letter "O"s that just touched the top and bottom lines of our note pads. The real challenge was when it had to be done not by a ball-point, but with an inkwell-dipped pen. And talking in class resulted in a recess or after-school period spent writing, "I will not talk in class" over and over and over. The greatest personal trauma for me was to make an 'r' so, according to the teacher, the rain would roll off the roof.

Then came the 1950s. Experts, led by Dr. Benjamin Spock, said all this was oppressive. Tight discipline didn't allow kids the freedom to "express themselves." Keeping kids after school was cruel and inhumane punishment. The result: While the experts take on other missions, young people can't even write legibly, much less construct sentences that begin with capitals and contain a subject, verb, and object. But the kids still are quite capable of expressing themselves; they tell their teachers to go to hell. Sometimes a teacher may object to such heady behavior, and this too often results in assault or even murder.

Back in 1913, another bunch of experts had decided to help manage the nation's money supply. They established the Federal Reserve Bank (FRB). Thanks to their help, the nation suffered the worst depression in its history and the greatest number of bank failures. And for good measure, they helped us attain a level of price instability unknown to pre-FRB America.

Now comes a new breed of experts doling out "innovative" advice. The Washington, D.C., government has just issued a proposal that such crimes as burglary, weapons offenses, and drug use not be punished by jail sentences. According to *The Washington Post,* Mark Cunniff, executive director of the National Association of Criminal Justice Planners, said, "Given the resource crunch people are experiencing, most are falling over themselves figuring out what they can do short of sending people to prison."

"Increasingly the issue of overcrowding and the cost of confinement is driving policymakers to rethink the issue of imprisonment," added Dale Parent, deputy director of the National Institute for Sentencing Alternatives at Brandeis University.

These experts would have us "rehabilitate" criminals by leaving them on the streets to prey on law-abiding citizens. Rehabilitation hasn't worked in prison, and it won't work on the streets. The experts tell us that, because of overcrowding, prisons are not safe. So they have to keep criminals out of jail; well, the reason the prisons are unsafe is because of the experts.

Years ago prison wardens came from the ranks of the prison guards. Prisoners thought thrice before they assaulted guards. Inmates didn't have access to loads of contraband. Furthermore, you didn't have the frequent escapes and riots that plague us today. Prison wardens today are college graduates, in other words, experts. With the help of the courts they've done seen to it that prisoners have all kinds of "rights": the right to rape, riot, murder, and escape. We don't need money and studies for our prisoners; we need to get rid of the experts and start applying some plain, old-fashioned common sense!

If the D.C. government proposal comes into practice, and burglary and weapons-carrying become non-jailable offenses, we should all start carrying guns. Meanwhile, I propose that we not listen to the "experts"; they've done a fine job of ruining the country. The common man is more to be trusted than any expert. The expert *thinks* he know's it all; but the common citizen realizes the folly of that misconception. And the common man has a greater sense of fairness. William F. Buckley once remarked that if he were on trial for his life, he'd rather the jury be selected at random from the Manhattan telephone directory than from the Harvard faculty list. Makes sense to me.

March 1985

Differing Visions and the Real World

HAVE YOU ever wondered how people of intelligence and goodwill can arrive at two entirely different conclusions after studying and observing the same evidence? It's all too easy, and unsatisfactory, to just impugn their motives. The best answer is that people often have different visions or assumptions about how the world operates.

Except for a handful of holdouts, people now believe the Earth is round. But at one time it was believed to be flat, and, of course, India couldn't be reached by sailing west. To people who held to the notion that the Earth was round, sailing west to reach India made good sense. Both groups thought the other evil, intransigent, and stupid. But both were following the logical dictates of their visions.

We still have problems of vision. And these are most difficult in the realm of social science, because faulty visions are not easily unveiled. In the physical sciences, it's relatively easy. Congress would be laughed out of existence if they enacted a bill which had as a precondition for its success the repeal of the law of gravity, such as: "Be it enacted that aircraft shall take off from New Jersey, shut off their engines, and henceforth proceed to California."

Yet Congress does pass bills which, in terms of stated objectives, require the repeal of the laws of supply and demand. Congress legislates increases in the minimum wage as a means to increase the income of the low-skilled worker. And Congress has a lot of support for such measures. Whether increases in the minimum wage law can improve the lot of the low-skilled workers depends on your vision. If you assume it takes a certain number of workers to do a job, that technology can't replace workers, and that when the price of something rises people use the same amount, it makes sense to argue for a higher minimum wage. After all, people will be better off getting $4.00 an hour than $2.00.

If, however, it is your vision that it *doesn't* take a certain number of workers to do a job (human dishwashers can be replaced by machines or disposable dishes) and that when the price of something rises people buy less of it, raising the legal minimum wage to $4.00 an hour as a means of helping the low-skilled, doesn't make sense. After all, being unemployed with the hypothetical right to $4.00 an hour buys fewer groceries than actually being employed at $2.00 an hour.

Another vision people have about economic life is that if people are allowed to charge, or pay, whatever price they wish, gouging exploitation and sin will rule the land. Possessed by that vision, Congress enacts all forms of law regulating prices in the "public interest." But the vision is wrong. Gasoline prices are now around $1.30 a gallon. Surely, gas station owners would find $3.00 per gallon a more pleasing price, and since there are no price controls why don't they? The answer is, they simply can't get away with it. While they're free to decide the price, we're free to decide the quantity we buy.

On a more personal basis, I'm free to tell Dr. George Johnson, president of George Mason University, "I now charge $200,000 a year for my professorial services." Knowing George, I'm afraid he'll say, "Great, Williams, I'll buy zero amount."

For the most part, our struggle is not between the forces of good and evil. It is really a conflict of visions and assumptions of how the world operates. None of us has the divine vision. Therefore, debate over nontraditional and heretical visions is necessary for the right idea. This is the great contribution of the Reagan administration. It has helped provide a climate for healthy vision testing.

July 1985

Education's Smoking Gun

In THE D.C. suburb of Alexandria, Virginia, school officials recently revealed that in grades one through eight black students trailed white students by between 29 and 42 percentage points on standardized national tests. In Prince Georges County, Maryland, another D.C. suburb, the disparity was twenty points. The National Commission on Excellence in Education found similarly disturbing data: nearly 47 percent of black seventeen-year-olds are functionally illiterate. These black/white statistics are dimmer yet when we consider that white academic achievement is grossly deficient.

Back in June 1980, a *Time* magazine cover story, "Help! Teacher Can't Teach," described teacher incompetence. A Chicago teacher told a reporter, "I teaches English." A Portland, Oregon, teacher, who received As and Bs in her education courses at Portland State University, was found to be functionally illiterate. Three-quarters of the Houston, Texas, teachers, who took a reading exam, failed it.

Reginald G. Damerall's book, *Education's Smoking Gun: How Teachers Colleges Have Destroyed Education In America* (Freundlich Books $17.95), tells it all. With insight, wit, and compassion, Damerall, a former professor of education at the University of Massachusetts, exposes the education establishment, particularly university education departments—the people who supposedly teach teachers to teach.

Damerall minces few words. Quoting Dr. Thomas Sowell, Damerall says "Schools and departments of education . . . [are] 'the intellectual slums' of the universities." He says, "Empty credentials are all that any school or department of education in any university gives to its graduates."

Damerall offers some personal evidence for his indictment. Mary, a candidate for a Masters Degree in Education (M. Ed.) at the University of Massachusetts, was in his class. She couldn't perform the simplest of assignments. Only after she had applied to the university's doctorate program did Damerall discover that Mary's Graduate Record Examination (GRE) scores indicated she did not have the intellectual capacity to organize and remember data. On the quantitative part of the test Mary scored 210 out of a possible 800. And her verbal score of 240 wasn't much better—especially when you realize that on GREs a student gets 200 just for writing his name (presumably, even if he gets it wrong). In effect, Mary scored zero, making her "innumerate" and semi-literate. Yet, she was granted an M. Ed. and is now possibly teaching.

Damerall cites the case of another student, Spencer, who was barely literate, yet won a teaching assistantship at the University's Communication Skills Center. Damerall protested, but the chairperson and the school's chief affirmative action lobbyist said, "I would advise you, Reg, *not* to exercise your integrity in this." Spencer was black.

Comedian Bill Cosby is always funny, even in the case of his doctorate in education. He's another U. Mass. product. U. Mass. solicited Cosby; and according to Damerall the degree he received has little relationship "to genuine academic achievement." Cosby, who grew up in the slums of North Philly with this columnist, is an exceptionally intelligent man with the smarts to earn a real degree. And the fact that he has a giveaway one, like some other celebrities, is harmless. He'll continue his brilliant career acting, telling jokes, and selling Jello instant pudding. But the Marys and Spencers are going to teach our children, and the joke's on us.

Damerall points out that teacher incompetency is not racial; his indictment applies to whites as well as blacks.

Education's Smoking Gun is serious, must reading. It's packed with evidence that should be the foundation for an official inquiry into educational fraud. While there are probably many reasons Johnny can't read, the one that Damerall exposes is a national scandal.

September 1985

Political Immorality

ARGUING THE merits of the Davis-Bacon Act of 1931, Congressman Miles Allgood (D.-Ala.) said, "That contractor has cheap colored labor that he transports, and he puts them in cabins, and it is labor of that sort that is in competition with white labor throughout the country," (*Congressional Record*, 1931, page 6513).

The Davis-Bacon Act calls for the payment of "prevailing wages" on all federally financed or assisted construction. The Secretary of Labor usually determines it to be the union wage or higher. Economists conclude that Davis-Bacon discriminates against non-union labor. Thus, it heavily discriminates against blacks because they are less likely to be in the construction craft unions. While the present rhetoric in support of Davis-Bacon has been modified, it still has a racially discriminatory effect.

The U.S. Attorney General and the President are calling for changes in Executive Order 11246 which gave rise to racial quotas. They correctly argue that quotas are offensive to the principles of fair play. But the problem is the play is not fair. Davis-Bacon and many other federal, state, and local laws rig the game against blacks. And members of the Reagan administration are not blind to this fact.

So the question is: Why would the administration call for an end to racial quotas while leaving untouched those very laws that discriminate against blacks? There are several possibilities: (1) They don't believe all the evidence about the discriminatory effects; (2) they don't care about the effects; or (3) it's the political hardball of counting votes. Other possibilities exist but they are even less flattering.

While the Reagan administration is of little help in providing an atmosphere of fair play, black congressmen are worse. As handmaidens of labor unions, these House members consistently vote the union position on any proposal to either reduce the restrictive effects of the Davis-Bacon Act or change other laws so as to improve employment opportunities for blacks. The payoff is that the unions support the campaign efforts and legislative agenda of the black congressmen who, in turn, support the union agenda.

The civil rights organizations, like the black lawmakers, think what's good for unions is also good for blacks as a group. They ignore the admonition of one of the earliest civil rights leaders, W.E.B. Du Bois who called unions the ". . . greatest enemy of the black working man." At the time Du Bois, Booker T. Washington, and other civil rights leaders expressed those concerns, unions were openly racist. No craft unions currently have racial restrictions in their charters, but what they do has a racial impact. When unions, through Davis-Bacon, can mandate $16 an hour for a carpenter, the carpenter whose skills make him qualified and employable at $9 an hour becomes ineligible for the job.

If black politicians had strategic smarts, they'd press the administration on this and similar issues. They should demand that if goals, numbers, and timetables are going to be removed so must restrictions like Davis-Bacon and numerous restrictive occupational licensure and labor laws.

The people at the Justice Department know these laws are government-backed collusions in restraint of trade. They say that to intervene with state and local monopolistic restrictions violates the principles of federalism. Nonsense! It's not a matter of federalism. It's a matter of the "due process" clause of the Fourteenth Amendment.

Maybe it's too much to ask that politicians rise above expediency and claim the moral highground. Morality and politics may be mutually exclusive.

December 1985

Real Compassion Is Hard

COULD YOU watch your child go off to school several days in a row, without lunch money, and come home starving? My mother did. Let's get to the why.

Deserted by my father, I lived in the slums of North Philadelphia with my mother and sister. Mom was a domestic servant and I supplemented the family income with after-school and weekend jobs. In addition to helping out at home, I was responsible for buying my own school lunches. Anybody with a fourteen- or fifteen-year-old knows about their financial discretion. Somehow by mid-week my lunch money was spent. Like clockwork, every Wednesday or Thursday I went to Mom to borrow lunch money until I got paid.

One week Mom said, "You knew you had to buy lunch when you spent the money." My impassioned pleas fell on the deaf ears of a mother I thought was the meanest, most callous person on the face of this earth. But it *never* happened again.

In my parental responsibilities, I wonder if the same amount of courage can be summoned. Surely it must be heart-rending to see your kid come home starving. But if you're going to be a good parent, you've got to find the guts to instill accountability.

A recent visit to Newark, New Jersey, reminded me of this childhood episode. I was invited by a religious organization (that prefers anonymity) working to revitalize people and property in ghettos. They purchased an abandoned school to provide private education. They purchased abandoned houses and fixed them up to rent to poor black ghetto residents. They started factories and other job training facilities for the poor. They're not doing anything on a grand national scale, but what they do is thoughtful and meaningful. What's more, the organization is committed to Christian principles of morality and charity; they refuse government money.

Standing out in stark relief at the Newark housing rehabilitation sites was the absence of black workmen. The director said job offers of $4.00 and $5.00 an hour were made to community residents, but they either wouldn't take the job or, if they did, couldn't be counted on to show up every day. These were low-skill apprentice labor jobs. White union workers from the suburbs must be hired to do the work.

Five dollars an hour translates into $10,000 per year. But that's before taxes and the expense of going to and from work. As such, it may not compare favorably with cash and benefits from an assortment of unemployment compensation and welfare programs. But that's a *short* run comparison. Taking a low-pay job means developing skills that might command a higher *future* income.

In the name of national compassion we've made dependency economically attractive. One solution is to put Mom in charge of welfare handouts. I can just see her telling somebody, "You knew you had to eat when you refused that $5.00 an hour job." Believe me; the specter of starvation is a powerful inducement to get your act together.

One of the greatest signs of the Judeo-Christian ethic of Americans is their great desire to help their fellow man. Testament to this is the fact that 80 percent of all giving in the world is by Americans. But we forget the most important question we must ask when helping someone: "What is the effect of our help on that person's own incentive to help himself?" The plight of the increasing number of dependent people begs that we ask that question.

February 1986

135

Freedom: Understand It
—or Lose It

THE PRESIDENTIAL Commission on Excellence in Education tells us that, unless something is done about our children's academic performance, we risk losing our scientific and technological preeminence. A far greater danger is that we risk our freedom, because the next generation has little understanding of the struggles that have made us truly unique.

The Declaration of Independence says, "We hold these truths to be self-evident, that all men are created equal, that they are endowed by their Creator with certain inalienable Rights, that among these are Life, Liberty and the pursuit of Happiness." Try asking a high school or college student the meaning of that statement. They *might* know its author: Thomas Jefferson. But ask them what writers influenced Jefferson's thinking. If you told them Aristotle, Locke, and Sidney, they might think you were talking about a rock band.

Anybody can forget names and places so let's be a bit charitable on that point. But what about those "inalienable Rights"? Were Jefferson, Patrick Henry, Thomas Paine, and others, talking about food stamps, housing subsidies, and welfare payments? No, they were saying precisely the opposite. Each person is precious; he has rights no one is entitled to breach. Each of us is entitled to serve his *own* purposes. It is the function of government to protect us from being used as an instrument to serve someone else's purpose. If you doubt you're being so used, take a look at your paycheck: check out the difference between what you agreed to work for and what you get.

Ask your youngsters what the Founders meant by "majority rule." They'll probably spout some nonsense like, "The majority of voters, or the will of the people, should decide what each of us is able to do." Nonsense! The Founders held the government should be democratic *only* in the sense of broad citizen participation, not in the political sense of majority rule.

It was precisely this concern—tyranny by the majority—that led Jefferson to insist on the adoption of the Virginia statutes, written largely by George Mason, into the Constitution as the Bill of Rights. The Bill of Rights specifically bans majority rule on several precious freedoms like speech, religion, and rights to property.

Of course the Founders made moral mistakes. The main one was not outlawing slavery. But a number of the Founders were either abolitionists or men who agonized over the issue, including Paine and Jefferson. While slavery was one moral problem, there was another identified by Alexis de Tocqueville in his classic, *Democracy in America,* written after his visit to the United States in 1830. It would be entirely unreasonable to expect today's high school or college student to know about this writer.

Tocqueville accurately anticipated America's current problem: " . . . but there exists also in the human heart a depraved taste for equality, which impels the weak to lower the powerful to their own level, and reduces men to prefer equality in slavery to equality in freedom." Tocqueville wasn't condemning equality before the law. He was talking about today's interpretation of equality before the law, which has been to mandate equal outcomes, wherein our Supreme Court claims, much as the Dodo in *Alice in Wonderland,* "Everybody has won, and all must have prizes."

July 1986

Free-Market Conflict Reduction

THE HISTORY of man is one of relentless conflict. We fight about religion, land, ethnicity, language, politics, or any other difference—real or imagined.

Picking a fight is easy; the big question is: What can we do to live together in relative harmony? As a start, we might try to let the free market allocate resources.

The free market reduces human conflict, while the political arena enhances it. The reason is that when we spend dollars, we are more likely to get more of what we want than when we vote for a politician. In other words, when you buy a pair of shoes—in effect, vote with dollars—you get a pair of shoes. When you vote for a politician, you don't know what you'll get.

Education provides us with a prime example of how conflict can be reduced through the free market. Some parents want busing, high school sex clinics, and exotic curricula, while many other parents strongly oppose these things.

A new conflict in that battle is being waged by Knoxville, Tennessee, parents in the U.S. District Court. The case, *Mozert et al.* v. *Hawkins County School System,* has been tagged by the media as another "Scopes Monkey Trial."

The plaintiffs, Christian Fundamentalist parents, object to the materials being presented to their children in the Holt, Rinehart & Winston elementary reading series. They object to theories of evolution being presented as fact. They object to the books presenting the occult and other religions while ignoring Christianity. The parents also object to what they see as an anti-American bias in the books their children are compelled to read. The court is scheduled to hear final oral arguments on September 24.

One doesn't have to take sides to recognize that parents, more than anyone else, should have the right to choose what their children are taught. Parents are responsible enough to choose clothes, food, doctors, and dentists for their children; they should also be able to decide what is good for them—daily prayer, sex education, the teaching of creationism and evolution—in the classroom. If individual parents shouldn't have the right to make such decisions, who should?

When schools are government-run, parents are denied such choices. There are either going to be prayers or no prayers. This means parents favoring prayers in school will inevitably butt heads with those who do not. Using political pressure, one group of parents will try to impose its wishes on the other. If those parents wishing school prayer lose, they will either have to accept a ban on prayers in school, fight back, or send their kids to a non-government school. To add insult to injury, the losing parents, who opt out of public school, will not only have to pay tuition, but also be forced to pay for the government schools for which they have no use.

Imagine all the conflict there'd be if we managed food, cars, and clothing the way we manage schools. You like Buicks and jeans, while I like Volvos and three-piece suits, but we don't have to fight each other in order to satisfy our personal preferences. You buy what you want, and let me buy what I want. Instead of fighting over these differences, we can watch tennis and drink beer together.

Why should education be any different? If we're going to have publicly financed schools, why not give each parent a cash-equivalent school voucher (school stamps)? That way parents could choose whatever school pleases them. The guy down the street could choose a school with an exotic curriculum while I stick with the basics and on Saturdays we could still have that beer together.

The market is not a utopia, but it serves people's varied wants and interests, and it reduces human conflict far better than government does.

September 1986

Let's Get Back to Basics

Hardly a day goes by without news stories on narcotics, teen pregnancy, juvenile delinquency, and crime. The average citizen responds by saying, "There ought to be a law." And—quite predictably—the average politician says, "There ought to be a program." I say we ought to get back to basics. Let's think about it.

Most civilized and responsible conduct does *not* result from acts of Congress. It comes from customs, traditions, and taboos. In a word: socialization. It's impossible for Congress or state lawmakers to regulate every aspect of individual conduct to make it civilized and responsible. In fact, a considerable part of uncivilized conduct may well be caused by Congress. For example, Congress has convinced many Americans that they have the right to live off other Americans via food stamps and welfare. Official recognition of such a "right" leads them to snatch your pocketbook. If caught, the thief could plead he's cutting government costs by eliminating the need for the IRS to collect and Congress to distribute.

The civilizing influence of customs, traditions, and taboos has been under relentless attack for decades and we shouldn't be surprised by the results. When I was growing up, for a girl to give birth without the benefit of marriage was a disgrace—for her, for her family, and, most unfortunately, for the baby who was labeled a "bastard." Today, this term, in reference to a baby, has become outdated.

Regardless of what we might think of the taboo, it acted as a strong sanction against reckless premarital sex. Moreover, once a girl did become pregnant, there were efforts to make the man do the "right" thing. They called it a shotgun wedding. That's become a thing of the past. Today, the girl marries the government, and the father's name is Mr. Welfare. Actually, it's you and me. I don't know about you but my IRS Form 1040 suggests that I support four families plus buy my share of the missiles. To add insult to injury, I don't even get a Father's Day card from my many families.

And what about today's unruly behavior by kids, which includes narcotics usage, property destruction, murder, and rape? Congress can't solve this problem, but customs, traditions, and taboos used to hold youthful exuberance in check. When I was a youngster, the school principal and teachers were, if not God, His close associates. It never occurred to us, in a dream or otherwise, to curse the teacher, much less stab or rape her. I remember one of the frequent times Mom was summoned to school to discuss why I was misbehaving in class. As the teacher was commenting on my non-studious behavior, I made the mistake of saying, "No, I didn't." Before the word "didn't" cleared my lips, and without benefit of due process, my head was reeling from a smack by Mom, who then asked whether I was calling the teacher a liar.

Today's kids have been "adultified." They have rights. Congress has sponsored American Civil Liberties Union activities to insure that principals employ due process. That means they can't force a kid to empty his pockets, or search his locker for guns or narcotics without a warrant. In the name of free speech, principals cannot enforce dress codes or civilized language in the school newspaper.

And there are attendance problems; some schools have 35 to 50 percent absentee rates. Kids have always played hooky, but you used to have to do it by hiding to steer clear of questioning adults and truant officers. Today? No problem. Kids play hooky and lounge around shopping malls and downtown video game arcades without fear of an official challenge: "How come you're not in school?"

We don't need lawmakers to get us back on the track of civilized conduct. What we *do* need to do is to prevent official sanctions from being levied against those institutions, customs, traditions, and taboos that have served us well. During the 1960s and 1970s rush to let it all hang out, we canned many institutional supports to civilized conduct and individual accountability. Now we reap the reward.

The solution is not for Congress to *do* something; the solution is for Congress to stop undermining our institutions, customs, traditions, and taboos.

October 1986

Nobel Prize Economist Underlines U.S. "Idea" Market

W<small>E'VE DONE</small> it again! Of the 18 Nobel Prizes that have been awarded to economists, Americans have been the winners 14 times. What's most exciting for me is that this year's winner is James M. Buchanan, professor of economics, at *my* school, George Mason University—just 13 miles from the nation's capital—in suburban Fairfax, Virginia.

Although he's a native of Tennessee, Buchanan's spiritual home is Virginia, where my great grandparents were slaves. But we didn't meet in Virginia. We met in 1968, nearly 3,000 miles away, at UCLA. He was a visiting professor, and I was a Ph.D. student.

Those were troubled times on the nation's campuses. Students were rioting and taking over buildings to protest racial discrimination and the Vietnam War. Even though I disagreed with some of their tactics, I had some sympathy for the objectives of the campus liberals.

Into this setting pops a demanding, uncompromising James Buchanan to teach courses in Public Finance. Buchanan's rigid style was no big problem for me. Living under my mother's roof I had become accustomed to that kind of training. The problem was Buchanan's being demanding, uncompromising, and rigid with a dignified southern drawl. I had been with enough southern boys in the Army to know that this spelled trouble.

The long and short of it all is that I was wrong. We hit it off quite well. Not only did we have a good exchange of ideas in class, but I passed his merciless Ph.D. preliminary exam. Moreover, there is something basically decent about people who are in their office, ready to work, at 6:30 in the morning. And we've enjoyed that same good relationship over the years, despite his erroneous claims that he taught me everything I know.

Professor Buchanan won the Nobel Prize for his path-breaking work in analyzing the economics of politics, a field known as Public Choice. His hypothesis is that politicians and bureaucrats do not lose their self-interested behavior upon assuming public office or attaining civil servant status. What does change are the restraints they encounter; that's the "bottom line." Many of our national problems are a direct result of politicians not having a bottom line. The benefits and costs of private decisions are focused and concentrated. In other words, if you don't maintain your house, you lose; you don't get as much when it's sold. If you maintain it, you win; you get more if you re-sell.

In politics, it's an entirely different story. If a politician or bureaucrat wastes national resources, the cost is spread over the entire nation. If he makes good decisions, the benefit is similarly dispersed. This produces socially perverse incentives. The "best" time to waste money is when it belongs to somebody else. And the best time to save is when it's your own. When politicians spend, guess whose money it is?

Buchanan's analysis suggests it's a waste of time trying to elect "good" politicians because everybody will behave roughly the same when faced with the same restraints. It's like gravity. Republicans fall at 32 feet per second squared, and so do Democrats. In Buchanan's less uncompromising moments, he might recommend we change the rules to give politicians greater private incentives to act in the national interest. Buchanan would be a strong advocate for a spending limit being written into the Constitution.

Yes, Buchanan is a great scholar. What's greater is the freedom we Americans have in the marketplace of ideas. It's this freedom that produces great scholars and explains why we walk away with most of the Nobel Prizes.

October 1986

Another Failed Miracle

OVER THE last twenty-five years, the federal government has spent well over $100 billion in more than 50 job training programs. The result: Unemployment among the targeted groups has soared. Politicians, bureaucrats, and professionals give us one sham story after another about the successes of their "cure" but never get down to the bottom-line question: Why has unemployment among the targeted groups risen?

James Bovard, writing for the Cato Institute, one of Washington's brightest think tanks, discusses government programs, "The Failure of Federal Job Training." The U.S. Department of Labor (DOL) leads the sham brigade with its strained definition of success. DOL calls a Job Corps trainee "employed" if he has had a job interview and counts trainees as permanently employed if they've spent one day on the job. In the eyes of DOL a major program achievement is teaching 17-year-olds to make change from a dollar.

In 1973, Congress passed the Comprehensive Employment and Training Act (CETA). CETA spent $30,000 to build an artificial rock for the training of rock climbers, gave $500 a month to a Communist organizer in Atlanta, paid for nude sculpture classes in Michigan, and doled out millions for other nonsense.

Like other government programs, CETA was fraught with fraud. Thirty-three Philadelphia Democratic party committeemen or their relatives were on the CETA payroll. Chicago CETA applicants needed a referral letter from ward leaders or their applications would be trashed. Nearly one-half of the Washington, D.C., City Council staff was on the CETA payroll.

Part of CETA's $53 billion was used to soak the taxpayers for more money. CETA money was used in Florida to hire people to go door-to-door persuading people to apply for food stamps. Maryland CETA workers chauffeured welfare recipients to the welfare office. New York CETA workers ran a phone service to let people know about their unemployment and welfare benefits.

CETA not only wasted money; it wasted human lives. Bovard points to several CETA evaluation studies that show: "Participation in CETA results in significantly lower post-program earnings." "All program activities have negative effects for men." "Significant earnings losses for young men of all races and no significant effects for young women."

During the Reagan years little has changed. In this year's Summer Youth Employment Program (SYEP), Washington teenagers busied themselves building a model cardboard city, or attending "Basketball Reading Incentive Camp." Many kids were routinely sent home hours before their "work day" ended. Others were bored to death with endless lectures about South Africa and nuclear power. In Baltimore, teens were paid to pass out toys and to chauffeur cats and dogs to old folks' homes. Last summer, Phoenix kids painted cars on the sides of buildings under the summer employment program.

In nearly all the federal job training programs, trainees are taught attitudes and habits that have little or nothing to do with success in a private sector job. They learn to keep out of the way, to come to work late, and to leave early.

The best way to create jobs is to abolish minimum wage laws, lower Social Security and other taxes that artificially raise the cost of hiring the low-skilled, and eliminate stifling business regulation. Then, reduce unemployment compensation, food stamps, and other handouts to able-bodied people so that people take those jobs that are available.

October 1986

Chapter V

INTERNATIONAL ISSUES

THE 1980s saw the emergence of several important international issues. The most important of them are the Strategic Defense Initiative, South African apartheid, and terrorism.

Tragically, for the survival of the world's democracies, new trade-offs against national defense have been discovered. Instead of basing our national defense on a realistic assessment of the Soviet threat, more and more Americans see national defense as a threat to the federal government's ability to manage and expand social welfare programs. Adam Smith's dictum of "defense before opulence" has been stood on its head. As the federal government takes on more and more illegitimate functions, national defense, as a percentage of its budget, has fallen over the last twenty years from 49 percent to 26 percent and has only reversed its downward spiral during the Reagan administration.

South Africa has emerged as the world's pariah nation. American abhorrence of South Africa's codified racial discrimination against blacks speaks well of our commitment to human rights. However, our policy toward South Africa is less than an intelligent method of breaking down apartheid.

We must recognize that South Africa is a sovereign nation. That means we have limited ability to control its domestic policy. We need to understand the true state of affairs in South Africa. Blacks in South Africa, particularly urban blacks, have the highest standard of living in sub-Saharan Africa. Over a million blacks from neighboring countries come to South Africa to work and earn a living much higher than that at home. Moreover, South Africa has the same problem along its borders we have along ours with Mexico—illegal aliens. Blacks from Mozambique, Zimbabwe, Botswana, and Zaire *voluntarily* leave their own country to live and work in South Africa. They do not come to vote; they come to earn. Blacks in South Africa have more cars, televisions, and other consumer goods, per thousand, than citizens of Russia. The per capita income of urban blacks is nearly $1600, well above the per capita income of $300 in the People's Republic of China.

The fact that black South Africans are better off than many other people does not mean that apartheid is any less detestable. It does mean South African blacks *can* be worse off than they are now. That fact forces us to ask whether our policy toward South Africa is going to *help* or *hurt* blacks. If blacks cannot be made worse off, then any half-baked policy will do.

Terrorism is something that free and open societies have great difficulty in combatting. It is a bit easier for us to respond adequately to terrorism when it is state-sponsored. We simply retaliate against the state, as we did with Libya.

Response to terrorist organizations not sponsored by states is far more difficult. At the minimum, we should not give in to demands; we should remove the Watergate-era shackles from intelligence agencies so there can be greater infiltration of terrorist organizations; and our military should continue its development and training of special anti-terrorist squads.

The columns in this section address themselves to these and other issues of international and foreign policy.

Beware the Well-Intentioned

SHOULD THE United States and other Western nations pursue a policy of disinvestment in South Africa? The answer depends on who you ask. American liberals, and other well-meaning people, from the safety and comfort of their high-rise apartments, say yes. I am sure they sleep better after taking a moral stance against trade with the devil.

But if you ask South African blacks, the supposed beneficiaries of disinvestment, you get a different answer. Chief Gatsha Buthelezi, leader of the Zulus, says no. The chief has told me, "Americans have got the whole issue exactly upside down. It is morally imperative that American firms remain active here." The chief's sentiments are shared by Lucy Mvubelo, general secretary of South Africa's largest union, David Thebehali, mayor of Soweto, and many others.

While the majority of black South African leaders are against disinvestment and boycotts, there are tiny factions that support disinvestment—namely terrorist groups such as the African National Congress.

What about the attitudes of independent black nations that surround South Africa? Official rhetoric is one thing. What they do is another. Black nations who vote for boycotts and deny South African Airlines the right to fly over their states conduct robust trade relations with South Africa. For example, each year South Africa receives 60,000 guest workers from Mozambique, 32,000 from Botswana, 21,000 from Zimbabwe and other countries plus many illegal entrants.

Western foreign investment in South Africa is significant; it totals $25 billion. South Africa, for its part, supplies the West with gold and diamonds and strategic minerals such as chrome, cobalt, manganese, platinum, and vanadium. A boycott of these exports would be devastating to several key Western industries.

South African problems defy simplistic solutions put forward by supporters of disinvestment and boycott. Ethnically, the country is diverse. It is not solely an issue of blacks versus whites. There are at least 17 different black ethnic groups. Several of which, like the Zulu and the Xhosa, have a centuries-old history of hostility. Black rule is no guarantee that the mass of South African blacks will be freer and have a higher standard of living. It could mean less, as the history of other African nations suggests.

Just a casual visit to South Africa demonstrates the enormity of the problem. Most blacks have no education in the Western sense. I've seen men being tutored in the use of a shovel. If the South African government would give its black countrymen freedom tomorrow, it would take well over 100 years before there would be meaningful equality.

South Africa's legalized discrimination is offensive to nearly every American. In fact, it's offensive to an ever-increasing number of white South Africans. Many of its labor laws are written for the express purpose of protecting whites from job competition with blacks. South Africa's minimum wage law and equal-pay-for-equal-work law have wide support among its racist unions because it will cost a company just as much to hire a black as to hire a white. Thus, fewer blacks will be hired.

In evaluating apartheid we might ask, how effective are the laws? Despite apartheid law, there is widespread evasion and contravention. Businesses illegally hire blacks. Some companies get around job reservation laws by changing job titles. Blacks are not permitted to live in cities such as Johannesburg. But if a census were taken in Johannesburg, blacks would probably outnumber whites. The question never asked about apartheid law is: If whites would not hire blacks, rent to blacks, buy or sell to blacks, why in the world would there be a need for a law? After all, elephants flying around would pose an air traffic hazard, but we don't need a law against them. The existence of apartheid law suggests whites would make economic transactions with blacks. The reason is that it is in their economic interest.

Economics has a way of bringing people to their senses. South Africa has been experiencing considerable economic growth. The increased demand for labor cannot be filled by its tiny white population. Businessmen, who need labor, search for and train black Africans, seek government exemptions from laws, and actually violate many racist laws.

Above all, it is South Africa's economic growth that is breaking the back of apartheid. Rapid economic growth makes racial discrimination costly. As such, this is the tragedy of the disinvestment movement. A growing, robust economy tends to reduce racial hostility and awareness; a declining or stagnating economy does the opposite. After all, can any sane person argue that American blacks could have just as easily achieved the social, political, and economic gains of the 1960s boom during the bust of the 1930s?

Blacks Hurt by Sanctions on South Africa

WELL, CONGRESS just returned from its summer recess. Of course, the nation would be better off if Congress extended its recess indefinitely. But that's neither here nor there. One proposed piece of legislation facing our national legislature is H.R. 1693, "Modifying Our Relations Toward South Africa," which is co-sponsored by Stephen J. Solarz (D.-N.Y.). The thrust of H.R. 1693 is to: (1) require U.S. companies, of more than twenty employees, located in south Africa, to have affirmative action programs; (2) ban all importation of Kruger-rands; and (3) prohibit U.S. banks from making loans to the South African government. The reasoning, I suppose, behind this legislation is to pressure South Africa as a means to get her to dismantle apartheid.

Pascal once said, "Men never do evil so completely and cheerfully as when they do it from a religious conviction." This thought characterizes much of the contemporary rhetoric and policy towards South Africa.

Even the most casual observer of South Africa's political-economic scene will agree that its government denies basic human rights to blacks in such areas as freedom of movement, employment, and equal protection under the law. However, consensus reached on present and historic injustices does not, itself, magically produce effective U.S. policy which helps South African blacks. We have to think.

H.R. 1693 is a mild form of disinvestment by comparison to others that have been proposed. But we need to ascertain whether any form of disinvestment is effective policy. First of all, U.S. direct investment in

152

South Africa is about $2 billion, or 16 percent of foreign investment, which amounts to about five percent of total investment. As a percentage, the U.S. investment in South Africa is not very important. However, it *is* important in South Africa's high-tech sector.

To the extent that foreign investment and trade produces jobs, black and white South Africans benefit from economic relations with the U.S. One target of Solarz' bill is South Africa's mining industry. That's too bad because mining is a source of job opportunity for over 500,000 blacks. South African mining, construction, and agriculture not only provide jobs for South African blacks but also for guest workers from neighboring countries. Blacks from the following countries work in South Africa: Mozambique (40,000), Zimbabwe (2,000), Malawi (15,000), Botswana (16,000). A large number also slip in illegally to work. These workers come to South Africa not seeking political rights, but a higher standard of living. In fact, black South Africans enjoy a standard of living which is about the highest on the continent.

South African blacks are indeed mistreated at the hands of the state. But if we're going to help, shouldn't we make sure our "help" doesn't hurt. Trade sanctions would hurt. In fact, most who might be called black leaders in South Africa are strongly against disinvestment. They are Gatsha Buthelezi, chief of the Zulus, Lucy Mvubelo, general-secretary of South Africa's largest union, David Thebehali, mayor of Soweto, Sam Motsuenyane, president of the National African Chamber of Commerce, and others. They all point to the fact that economic ties to the West improve the economic lot of blacks and break down the barriers of apartheid as well.

South Africa does not treat its black citizens justly, but does not have anywhere near the atrocious record of other black nations. Between 1974 and 1978, Ethiopia executed 30,000 people; the Burundi government killed 250,000 people; Idi Amin's Uganda massacred over 300,000 people, and the tale goes on without public outcry—and without Congressman Solarz proposing trade sanctions against these brutal governments. But, of course, that's *blacks* brutalizing *blacks,* which is okay in the minds of many both here and abroad.

There's an admonition given to medical doctors, *primun non noncere.* It means, "First do no harm," which we would be well advised to heed in our policy toward South Africa.

October 1983

153

Socialism Plagues Africa

SOUTH AFRICA is in the news again. The House has passed a resolution calling for mild sanctions. And the Senate stands ready to vote on that resolution which prohibits new sales of Krugerrands and requires American firms in South Africa to implement affirmative action programs.

South Africa is in many respects a sad country. Sad chiefly because of its unrealized potential to be the garden spot of the continent. In 1980, this writer spent two months there and lectured at nearly all of its universities and before major groups. The complete story of South Africa is never told to the American people.

South Africa, according to its official rhetoric, is a capitalistic country. This claim is not merely a lie, it's a pernicious lie. On South Africa's government-owned television, I pointed out that its leadership is ignorant of the economic definition of socialism, which is, government ownership and/or control over the means of production. In South Africa, the government owns coal-to-oil conversion plants, railroads, the telephone company, and other major industries. Through licensing and regulation it controls all enterprises from banks, gold mines, and insurance companies to supermarkets. It even tells its citizens *when* they may buy toilet tissue, soap, and dog food. I suggested to the interviewer that if the government could somehow convert the world's avowed socialists to Chistianity they would find a nearly ready-made home in South Africa.

The problem with this official lie is that black South Africans speak out against capitalism and for socialism, and who can blame them? In numerous conversations with blacks during my visit I'd ask: "Do you think you should have the right to go into business without getting permission?" "Yes." "Do you think you should be able to purchase property where you want?" "Yes." "Do you think your job, and the conditions thereof, should be left up to you and your employer?" "Yes." "Yes" answers to these and similar questions show the person is really *for* capitalism and free enterprise. Ironically, socialism, which many blacks say they believe in, with all of its controls and interferences with voluntary exchange, has victimized and continues to victimize black South Africans.

But black South Africans are not the only victims of South African socialism. White people are as well. White businessmen would love to hire more blacks but the law thwarts them in the name of maintaining "labor peace." Racist labor unions and other vested interests use government to get laws written which bar blacks from competing.

Blacks are not allowed to open businesses in white areas. But there's equal lack of opportunity. Whites are not allowed to open businesses in black areas either. Not widely known is the fact that whites do not present a united front in South Africa. There is considerable animosity between the politically strong Afrikaners and the economically strong English. The Afrikaners readily recall the Boer War where the English used concentration camps to brutalize their women and children.

The solution to South Africa's problem lies mostly in the creation of a state where there is freedom of human action, in a word, capitalism. Sadly enough "humanitarians," who say they want to help the blacks, press for more socialism. They merely wish to change the color of the dictator.

The most constructive step the South African government can make is to own up to the fact that it is a socialistic regime. In fact, socialism is the number one enemy of the entire continent of Africa. It fosters a parasitic relationship between the elite and the commoner.

February 1984

Crusaders Who Don't Look Back

Lᴇᴛ'ꜱ ʀᴇꜰʀᴇꜱʜ our memories. In April 1979, elections were held in Rhodesia, now called Zimbabwe, where for the first time the nation's 7 million blacks had the right to vote. This election produced a multiracial government under the leadership of Bishop Abel Muzorewa.

The British government rejected the election. Under pressure from the Congressional Black Caucus, the U.S. government followed suit. Joined by the NAACP, the National Urban League, and Randall Robinson, executive director of Transafrica, black congressmen said Bishop Muzorewa's election was nothing more than a racist solution to the problems of Rhodesia. They demanded U.S. sanctions remain in force against the new south African nation.

They condemned any political solution that didn't include guerrilla leaders Joshua Nkomo and Robert Mugabe, who were fighting the Ian Smith regime in Rhodesia from Marxist bases in Mozambique and Zambia. A second election was held, and Robert Mugabe, a self-proclaimed Marxist, became prime minister. His Western backers, including America's black politicans and civil rights spokesmen, were ecstatic. They said Mugabe would be a statesman and that full participatory democracy was just around the corner in Zimbabwe. Further, they held, Zimbabwe's success at majority rule would become a model for change in South Africa.

Well, Robert Mugabe has consolidated power, but Zimbabwe is not the country predicted by his Western supporters. Interviewed by Allan Brownfeld, in *The New York Tribune* (4/25/84), the Reverend Sithole, a longtime black nationalist leader, said Zimbabwe is rapidly becoming an authoritarian state where any opponents of Mugabe are imprisoned. The press is being silenced. Bishop Muzorewa has been jailed. Opposition parties are not allowed on television or radio. And Mugabe has organized youngsters, ages 14 to 18, into a Youth Brigade. In addition to their job of reporting suspicious members of their own families, these teenagers instill fear throughout the land—burning Bibles, torching cars, and disrupting church services.

At higher levels, Mugabe's North Korean-trained Fifth Brigade slaughters any potential political opponents, particularly Ndebele tribesmen, traditional enemies of the Shona, Mugabe's tribe. According to Amnesty International, Mugabe's Fifth Brigade brutally beat, bayoneted, and killed hundreds of civilians in Matabeleland North in January 1983. According to the Reverend Sithole, there are thousands of political prisoners in Zimbabwe. Zimbabwe's Attorney General Chiyausiku recently said that rules of evidence will be amended to allow confessions obtained through torture to be admissable in court.

While these gross human rights violations are a part of the daily life of Zimbabweans, there's a deafening silence among the Congressional Black Caucus, the NAACP, and the Urban League. With all of Jesse Jackson's "love" for Third World people, we've heard *nothing* from him about the atrocities in Zimbabwe. These crusading "civil rights" turkeys are riding blindly from cause to cause, never looking back to see the results of their last crusade. Right now, they're busy on their latest: El Salvador.

Of course, we could be wrong. They might feel that whites killing blacks violates human rights, while blacks killing blacks is okay. If that's the case, the black leadership's international policy is consistent with its domestic agenda.

May 1984

Socialism: Swedish Style

LAST MONTH'S vacation took us to Sweden, the classic welfare state. The Swedish government cares for its citizens from the day they are born 'til the day they die providing goodies like: *free* child care, *free* medical care, and, under certain conditions, *free* housing and transportation. If workers get sick, employers pay 100 percent of their wages for the first two days. A national health insurance program pays 90 percent of wages for the balance of the illness. A not-too-surprising result is rife absenteeism and, to no surprise, a payroll tax of 45 percent of worker wages levied on employers. Sweden also provides goodies for children. Spanking is illegal. A spanked child need only report it to authorities to have his guilty parent fined.

For Americans pressing for more government spending and industrial planning, Sweden is a good crystal ball. First, we must remember there's no free lunch. No government can give what it hasn't first taken. Our government takes a full 44 percent of what we produce each year. The Swedish government beats us by a full 50 percent, taking 67 percent of what Swedes produce each year.

The maximum marginal tax rate in Sweden is 70 percent. Most Swedes are in the 50 percent bracket, and that's on top of property taxes and a value added tax (VAT) of 20 percent levied on nearly all products. Then there is Swedish inflation, a hidden tax just recently lowered to 8 percent, and the hidden tax of a 12 percent government budgetary deficit. The government's appetite for spending isn't satisfied, nor can it be. Some members of Parliment have proposed, in light of increasing Swedish resistance to tax increases, there should be a law mandating "voluntary" social work for each Swede—things like running errands for the elderly, cleaning streets, and babysitting.

The Swedish response to high and ever increasing taxes is that of tax avoidance and outright evasion. Part of this tax avoidance can be seen by all the nice boats dotting the Swedish archipelago on a warm summer day. As in the U.S., a person can deduct home mortgage interest. Many Swedes take out a second mortgage on their homes to buy a boat. Others participate in a large, flourishing underground economy. And still others outright falsify their tax forms. As in the U.S., the Swedish government has turned otherwise honest, law-abiding people into criminals.

Once government oppression starts, it has a mind of its own; oppression breeds oppression. To keep money in Sweden, the government bans its citizens from purchasing stock in foreign-held companies. A Swedish citizen going abroad can take no more than 10,000 kroner, which at the current exchange rate is a little more than one thousand dollars. That means a nice vacation requires you sneak your money out. But you risk detection by specially trained money-sniffing dogs. Maybe the anticipation of a similar policy is the motivation for the recent talk that new U.S. money be made with metal strips so it can be sensed by metal-detection machines.

Americans can learn a lot from the Swedish experience. We should not seek comfort in the fact that our government only takes 44 percent of our earnings; on the way to 67 percent the Swedes went through 44 percent. We should not seek comfort in the political rhetoric of "taxes on business and corporations." That, too, is the rhetoric of the Swedish Social Democrats who levy taxes on businesses only to have the tax passed on to consumers in the form of higher and higher prices. Neither should we listen to calls for less military spending in exchange for more social spending. The Swedes spend vast amounts for social programs and cannot detect, much less prevent, Soviet submarines from violating their territorial waters to gather vital intelligence and land hundreds of Soviet KGB agents on their shores. What we should listen to are the combined lessons of private property and limited government that made us a nation of unprecedented prosperity, freedom, and strength.

September 1984

Kennedy in Africa

SENATOR EDWARD Kennedy (D.-Mass.) arrived in South Africa to a welcome he never expected. He was met by black demonstrators booing and chanting "Kennedy go home!" Nobel Laureate Bishop Desmond Tutu, the media-appointed spokesman for South African blacks, had invited Kennedy for a fact-finding trip. Poor Kennedy, how was he to know Tutu was not the spokesman for South Africa's sixteen or seventeen major tribes.

Irann Moosa, spokesman for the Azanian People's Organization, said, "Kennedy must be informed that the oppressed blacks of Azania (a black activist name for South Africa) are not his ticket to the presidency, and that our enemy includes the imperialists of United States." Another activist said, "We do not need Kennedy to choose our leaders for us. He is a capitalist and an imperialist."

Kennedy's reception reflects the diversity of opinion among South African blacks that is shielded from Americans. With the notable exception of a recent CBS *60 Minutes* show, Americans are taught the South African problem is simply one between monolithic blacks and monolithic whites. If Kennedy had wanted his boots licked to the bantering of "Amens" and "Right ons," he should have preached to the demonstrators at the South African Embassy in Washington.

In 1980, the Free Market Foundation of South Africa, an organization that promotes personal liberty and is headed by Mr. Leon Louw, an Afrikaner, invited me for a two month lecture tour. This afforded me the opportunity to lecture at nearly every university and meet with most major elements of the South African community. Private meetings were held with important people such as Gatsha Buthelezi, chief of the Zulus (who, by the way, just told Kennedy that disinvestment was insanity), Prime Minister Sebe of the Ciskei, and many others, including the political leaders of Namibia (Southwest Africa). Meetings were also held with members of the South African Parliament and Prime Minister Botha's cabinet. The visit left me impressed with the awesomeness of the problem, but also, the conviction that *if* it is solved, South Africa will be the garden spot of the continent.

Americans are led to believe the South African problem is solely one of blacks not having such rudimentary political rights as the right to vote and the right to equality before the law. Denial of these rights, basic to human decency, offends any freedom-loving person. But the South African problem runs much deeper. Even if the South African government eliminated its remaining apartheid laws, as it is being urged to do by many white South Africans, it would take decades before there would be anything close to socio-economic equality.

Without minimizing political disenfranchisement of South African blacks, their longer term problem is paucity of human capital. Human capital is what economists call education and other productive skills. With the exception of a few urban blacks, it is safe to say that most do not have the human capital that black Americans had at Emancipation. It is easy to blame the gross injustices of the past but it's harder to do what's necessary to improve the situation. The right to vote, alone, won't produce the human capital blacks need any more than it has in other African nations that never saw colonialization or have had long periods of independence.

Americans can constructively help black South Africans. We can keep the moral pressure on South Africa to give blacks legal equality. We can contact organizations like the Free Market Foundation of South Africa to find out where we can send contributions for education. We should support the continuance of on-the-job training by U.S. firms in South Africa.

Grandstanding for publicity and politics is easy. But the hard, heart-rending, sometimes frustrating job of actually helping people to become better off is real compassion.

January 1985

The Path to More

STARVATION IN Ethiopa, Chad, and Mozambique has claimed more than a half-million lives. Such human suffering is unspeakable and unnecessary, yet its full story goes untold.

Several years of drought have played a major role in the famine. And internal strife has eliminated a lot of agricultural activity, while the desert encroaches upon once useful land. There's been massive deforestation.

Television cameras are good at pinpointing the physical aspects of the tragedy. But they can't show the human organizational structures or institutions that play such a vital role in the determination of incentives. In other words, you can't get television pictures of abstractions like private property, communal property, profit motive, or savings and investment.

The economic problem throughout much of sub-Saharan Africa is government hostility toward both private property and freedom of individual initiative. A lot of hostility stems from Marxist ideology proclaiming the sins of profit, wealth accumulation, and private property. But private property and individualism have never been a strong part of African culture.

People trivialize the effects of weakened private property rights and attack the pursuit of profit in a rush to promote a more "compassionate" system, such as socialism or communism. It is amazing to see the

Mengistu regime (Ethiopia's Marxist leaders)—who say they want food for their people—imitate the Soviet agricultural system. That's like asking illiterates to help you perfect sentence structure.

Private ownership has many benefits, but its greatest benefit is that it gives people an inducement to behave in ways that raise the future value of property. People take better care of their own home than they would apartments or public housing.

Privately owned forests receive better care than publicly owned forests. People litter their privately owned land less than they do publicly owned places. Why people behave this way is simple. Private owners reap personal rewards for conserving and enhancing property values and obversely bear the burden for destroying its value. In the case of houses, people get a higher resale price for their homes if they take care of them.

Problems in Africa range from soil erosion to overgrazing to allowing the desert to reclaim agricultural land. Communally owned land is nobody's land. People who only *use* the land have little incentive to make private sacrifices to ensure that it remains productive. When the land becomes useless, they merely move on to another parcel of the "people's land."

Ethiopian Marxists say arbitrage and speculation are capitalist sins and hence outlaw them as hoarding. But Chicago futures arbitrage and speculation are essential to efficient production and distribution. Here's how it works. Much of Florida's citrus crop was destroyed by blight. Citrus prices shot up aided by speculators who bought the crop now to sell later in hopes of earning profits. However, higher prices gave California citrus growers, and foreign growers as well, incentive to harvest more and gave consumers an incentive to use less. Isn't that the ideal response to a calamity: Producers produce more and consumers use less? But price controls and other Marxist ideology inhibit swift corrective responses to natural tragedies. If our government had slapped price controls on citrus products, producers and consumers would have gone on as if nothing had happened.

Starving Ethiopians are victims of their own government more than the weather. A compassionate American response demands coping with the immediate problem of filling starving stomachs and treating disease. But the long-term solution requires that we ship Africans some good, old-fashioned agricultural capitalism to plant on their farms.

February 1985

What Have We Learned From the Holocaust?

PRESIDENT REAGAN'S controversial visit to a World War II German soldiers' cemetery and a concentration camp should give us pause to ask what we've learned from the Holocaust.

Unfortunately, little appears to have been learned from this tragic episode of man's inhumanity to man. As a result, we betray the sacred memory of millions who died in gas chambers and fighting Hitler.

Many of us are tempted to attribute the Holocaust to a defect in German moral character. However, prior to the collapse of the Weimer Republic, Germany was one of the most hospitable countries for Jews in their entire history of persecution. Jews were accepted. And while they comprised just one percent of the German population, they accounted for 10 percent of the doctors and dentists, 17 percent of the lawyers, and 27 percent of Germany's Nobel Prize-winners.

In America, German-Americans were among the first Abolitionists and were fervent supporters of Lincoln and the emancipation of blacks. Philosophers like John Stuart Mill, in writing about personal liberty, got much of their inspiration from German philosophers, such as Goethe and Humbolt.

With such a rich history of respect for liberty, the question is, what happened? Clearly, part of the answer is that Hitler was a maniacal racist. But maniacal racists are everywhere, including the U.S.

What happened in Germany was the rise of Marxist socialism. German scholars such as Fichte, Rodbertus, and Lassalle were not only the most important contributors to Naziism, but acknowledged fathers of socialism. According to them, the individual has no rights, just duties. Another socialist architect of Naziism, Lensch, said, "Socialism is coming . . . and to assist the growth of a new conception of State and Society . . . Socialism must present a determined opposition to individualism." In *Mein Kampf*, in praise of the Aryan, Hitler said, "[H]e willingly subordinates his own ego to the community. . . ."

While not word for word, we've all heard identical collectivist statements from American politicians, do-gooders, and most recently the Catholic bishops in their "Pastoral Letter," which said, "It is the very essence of social justice to demand from each individual all that is necessary for the common good."

The basic requirement of socialism—both the socialism of Hitler's National Socialist German Workers' Party or the socialism of Karl Marx (himself a German)—is the subordination of the individual to the state. This requires unlimited growth of government. One major reason for Hitler's success was that considerable collectivization had already taken place in the form of government control over unions, businesses, and other aspects of German life. Hitler's maniacal racism was not as successful as he would have liked, because the state machinery was not without its defects. Jews changed their names and otherwise disappeared. But if Hitler had an agency like our IRS, with its massive detailed information on all of us, Jewish extermination might have been complete.

Since World War II, there have been calls for bigger government, more controls, and abrogation of private property rights in America. Of course there's the temptation to say, "It can't happen here!" That's precisely what Bismarck, or a Jew living in Germany during the Weimer Republic, might have said.

America today is nothing like Nazi Germany. However, there are two important facts to remember: 1) Even if you take tiny steps in a direction, one day you'll get there; and 2) civility is fragile.

May we never forget what happened in Nazi Germany. May we never turn our backs on the lessons of history.

May 1985

Let's Look Before We Leap

COMPARED TO the freedoms we take for granted, South Africa's apartheid system is an abomination. As such, it richly deserves our moral condemnation. Unfortunately, the alternatives for blacks in South Africa appear *not* to be either the status quo or democracy. The history of the African continent suggests the real-world alternative to South Africa's apartheid may well be brutal oppression and slaughter. Such a suggestion is not an argument for the status quo, it's an argument for caution.

Let's look at some of the history of sub-Saharan Africa. Uganda won independence in 1962. But black rule didn't bring freedom and prosperity. Instead, under Idi Amin, more than 50,000 blacks were murdered. Since 1979, when Milton Obote took power, an estimated 100,000 Ugandan civilians have been killed. It remains to be seen what will happen now with the overthrow of Obote.

Guinea became independent in 1958. Its government destroyed freedom of speech and press and established political prisons. By 1984, more than one-fifth (1.5 million) of its population had fled into exile.

The same story of oppression and murder repeats itself whether it is in the newly formed government of Zimbabwe, Zaire, the Central African Republic, Mozambique, or the never-colonized Ethiopia. Even more tragic is the fact that under colonial rule, some African countries were better off both economically and politically. This observation is not a sanction of colonialism, just an unpleasant reminder that black rule, in and of itself, is no sure-fire guarantee of a better life for African blacks.

Whether knee-jerk do-gooders in the West will admit it or not, black South Africans already have a measure of freedom and prosperity envied elsewhere. Bishop Desmond Tutu appears on television, from South Africa, to condemn its government—then goes about his business. Can Bishop Abel Muzorewa or Joshua Nkomo do the same in Zimbabwe, or Lech Walesa in Poland, or Andrei Sakharov in Russia?

Unknown to most Americans is the fact that South Africa has problems at its border similar to those we have at our border with Mexico—illegal aliens. Already several hundred thousand blacks come to work in South Africa from the neighboring states of Botswana, Malawi, Zimbabwe, Mozambique, and Swaziland. These blacks entering South Africa are not seeking to vote; they're seeking a better standard of living. In fact, South Africa's urban blacks have the highest per capita income ($1500) in Africa. By contrast, per capita income in the People's Republic of China is $295.

So the issue should be: How can we build on what South African blacks already have? The history of Africa demonstrates all too vividly that things could be worse. The proposed policy of disinvestment and other economic sanctions represent the politics of frustration—doing *something* will make us sleep better. But will South African blacks be better off?

Economic sanctions carried to the extreme will not only reduce opportunities for South African blacks working in Western-owned companies but spell utter calamity to South Africa's neighbors. Little known is the fact that Zambia, Zaire, Kenya, Zimbabwe, and Mozambique conduct robust trade with South Africa in vital foodstuffs and transportation. If one travels to these countries, he is just as likely to see the label, "Made in S.A." as anything else. This points to the hypocrisy of black states that daily condemn Western economic ties to South Africa but themselves carry on a robust trade with the apartheid regime. Full economic sanctions may punish blacks much more than whites—a question uninteresting to American sanctioners.

Americans and other freedom-loving people must condemn South African apartheid. At the same time we must not be blind to the fact that our actions can make South African blacks worse off. The solutions to

Africa's problems go far beyond the mere installation of a black government to replace a white one. Furthermore, the West has a vital stake in South African stability. The Soviet Union would like nothing better than to capture the strategic Horn of Africa and deprive the West of South Africa's strategic minerals upon which we depend for our high-tech economy.

August 1985

Will They Ever Learn?

THE BREAKING story of a somewhat dull summer was the fortieth anniversary of the atomic bombing of Hiroshima and Nagasaki. Descendants of the 1930s peaceniks marched, whined, and second-guessed President Harry Truman's decision to use atomic weapons against Japan. It was the peaceniks of the 1930s who called for the Allies to disarm, claiming there was going to be "peace in our time." That meant we turned a blind eye to Adolph Hitler's adventures and massive military buildup in violation of the Treaty of Versailles. The weakness of our Pacific forces fed the expansionary visions of Japan. Our unpreparedness led to the bloodiest war in the history of man; now the peaceniks again ask us to go unprepared.

In important respects one has to doubt the sincerity and/or intelligence of the peaceniks' blame-America-first mentality. They hold no marches on December 7, the anniversary of Japan's brutal sneak attack on Pearl Harbor. They hold no ceremonies for the 200,000 Chinese civilians massacred in Japan's rape of Nanking. Not a single tribute for Manila hospital patients doused with gasoline and set afire by Japanese soldiers. They hold no moment of silence for war prisoners who died by starvation, in brutal death marches, or as bayonet practice-targets for Japanese soldiers. In comparison to Japan's inhumanity in World War II, the atomic bombing of Hiroshima and Nagasaki was an act of compassion.

The peaceniks ignore the fact that while the nuclear bombing of Japan took as many as 240,000 lives, it saved many times that number. U.S. troops had been scheduled to land on Kyushu and Honshu. General George Marshall estimated a cost of a quarter-of-a-million to a million U.S. casualties. On top of that, the invasion would have resulted in hundreds of thousands, if not millions, of dead Japanese—soldiers and civilians. The atomic bombing of Japan was necessary. As Truman said, we were dealing with a beast. Indeed, Japan's total, unquestionable defeat paved the way for it to become the prosperous, democratic nation it is today.

The fact that the atomic bomb brought the war to a speedy conclusion was beneficial to the Japanese in another way. It allowed Japan to be occupied solely by the United States. General Douglas MacArthur mandated that American occupation troops were to treat the Japanese humanely. By contrast, of the Japanese troops who surrendered to Russia in Manchuria, 350,000 were sent to Siberia's slave-labor camps. Had the war gone on longer, Russia would have occupied Japan *with* the United States. That easily could have meant a Tokyo Wall with Japanese on one side free and prosperous and on the other side poor and oppressed.

American peaceniks and their European allies, in their blame-America-first mentality, ignore other beasts. When they whine about "nuclear brutality," do we hear them mention the millions of Russians and Chinese slaughtered during the Stalinist and Maoist purges? What about Russia's brutal suppression of the Hungarians? There is no indication that we would not see repeats of these acts if the Russian and Chinese bosses deemed it necessary.

The unintended agenda of the peaceniks is to invite war. The surest route to war is to give Russia the slightest inkling it can win. The peaceniks and their friends in Congress are doing just that. Democratic societies in their quest for survival against totalitarian ones have a real handicap. In democratic societies, leaders have to pay attention to large, vocal groups who call for disarmament. In totalitarian societies, demonstrators can be ignored or sent to slave-labor camps. We must protect ourselves from those who'd risk our freedom by destroying our ability to defend ourselves merely for the sake of being able to use more of the budget for federal handouts.

August 1985

South African Phonies

THE REVEREND Jerry Falwell, leader of the Moral Majority, caused considerable consternation when he called South Africa's Bishop Desmond Tutu a phony. Falwell told only part of the story. At the conclusion of a two month South African lecture tour in 1980, the Barclays Bank Women's Executive Group invited yours truly to deliver a speech to a mixed audience in Johannesburg. I summarized my observations by telling the audience that South Africans deserve one another. That might have been a frustration-driven overstatement, but not by much. But it was my impression that few in South Africa—white or black—truly favor individual freedom.

In a September 1980 article in *Frontline,* called "Plastic Surgery Can't Change Its Ugly Face," Bishop Tutu said, ". . . I must say I am opposed to capitalism. . . ," because, he explained, it is part of what he sees as "an essentially exploitative economic order." The bishop concluded ". . . that no amount of plastic surgery can change its [capitalism's] ugly face."

On the other side, government officials, from President Pieter W. Botha on down, are quick to describe South Africa's economic order as "our free-enterprise system," saying the nation's fight is against socialism.

In an interview on SABC, South Africa's government-run television network, I said (to the interviewer's chagrin) that to refer to South Africa's system as capitalistic or free enterprise was wrong. South Africa's white officials have no idea of the economic meaning of socialism. But its economic meaning is simple; it means government ownership and/or control over the means of production. I suggested that since there was so much government ownership and control, if socialists could be converted to Christianity, they'd be quite comfortable in South Africa.

During my visit I encountered many blacks who said they like communism or socialism. I'd ask them: "Do you believe you should be able to live where you please? Do you believe you should be able to start a business where you please? Would you like to buy and sell land where you please? Should you be able to work, come and go, and marry according to your wishes?" Not one black South African answered no to any of the questions. They were laissez-faire capitalists—and didn't know it.

What black South Africans must fight is what they now have: The widespread control of a socialistic society. South Africa's labeling of its system as capitalism is not merely phony, it's stupid. It causes blacks, dissatisfied with the status quo, to call for socialism, failing to realize it's been their enemy all along.

For Bishop Tutu to say capitalism has an ugly face is nothing less than resolute ignorance. Countries that have the greatest measure of freedom and prosperity for their citizens are those closer to capitalism than communism. Citizens of Japan, West Germany, Hong Kong, and the United States enjoy precisely those freedoms black South Africans seek. How many freedoms are enjoyed by the highly controlled citizens of China, Russia, Nigeria, and South Africa?

The unrecognized tragedy in South Africa is the competition for power. Afrikaners (whites) want to keep power and privileges; blacks want to take them away. Government power is always power over people and, if abused, can be the source of great human suffering. The color of the power-brokers makes little difference. The evidence is overwhelming right there on the African continent. Power was transferred from white colonial masters to blacks in Zimbabwe, Uganda, Kenya, Mozambique, and the former Congo states; yet the brutality continues. Unfortunately, neither Desmond Tutu nor South Africa's white masters seem to understand the meaning of true freedom.

September 1985

A Day of Infamy

Forty-four years ago, December 7, 1941, Japanese forces conducted a brutal sneak attack on Pearl Harbor. A shocked nation, led by President Franklin D. Roosevelt, felt a great sense of loss and betrayal. After all, FDR's 1940 landslide reelection was won in some measure on the promise "to keep our boys out of the war." Prior to this promise, Japan occupied Manchuria and Shanghai. Italy had invaded Ethiopia, and Hitler had stormed into Austria and Poland. Neville Chamberlain, prime minister of England, a man of high administrative ability and an abhorrer of war, believed Hitler could be dealt with rationally by treaty. He told his nation that there would be "peace in our time." Chamberlain's proof was the 1938 Munich agreement with Hitler, which stated that Britain and Germany would settle their problems by consultation and never again go to war.

The costliest war in man's history got underway in earnest in 1941. When Roosevelt said, "Yesterday, December 7, 1941—a date which will live in infamy. . . ," he should have added, "signatures on a piece of paper are worthless as a means to keep the peace." Thinking that autographs on paper can keep the peace cost us nearly 300,000 American lives and another 700,000 wounded.

Is there any lesson from this to be learned by today's Americans who

173

seem to want a U.S./Soviet agreement at any price? Abundant historical evidence shows beyond a shadow of a doubt that the only deterrent to expansionist totalitarian desires is the knowledge that the price of expansion will be too high. The only thing that has held Soviet designs even remotely in check is the Soviets' knowledge that if they go too far, their homeland will glow a nice radioactive green.

But, like Hitler, the Soviets have discovered a technique that might give them a leg up. All the while Hitler was building a military machine for conquest, he sued for peace. He inked a treaty with Russia. He convinced England his designs were moderate and eminently reasonable. Thus he bought time to gear up his military machine.

With a similar plan the Soviets come to Geneva. Thanks to the Communist system, the Soviet economy is in shambles. While America's gullible peaceniks decry the feasibility of our Strategic Defense Initiative (SDI) (dubbed "Star Wars"), the Soviets have complete confidence in our technical competence. Realizing this, they, like Hitler, are at the arms-limitation table, buying time. And they have American allies—people on their side to help stifle progress on SDI.

Soviet "friends" in the U.S. are not friends in the true sense of the word. Rather they are unwitting accomplices to Soviet designs. We see them on the six o'clock news. Tip O'Neill wants more food stamps, so he attacks national defense expenditures. Tip thinks that to handle the deficit crisis it is just as legitimate to cut food stamps by 10 percent and the military by 10 percent, claiming all government programs should bear a "fair" burden of spending cuts. On any number of occasions, Secretary of Defense Caspar Weinberger has tried to explain to Congress that a sensible military budget is determined by the nature of the military threat, not some nonsense like fair share of the budget-cut sacrifice.

If President Reagan makes the kind of concessions to the Russians demanded by some Americans, including even some members of his cabinet, future generations will rightfully hold him in contempt.

But thinking back to the Day of Infamy, I wonder if the people who demonstrated last August 14, lamenting the atomic bombing of Hiroshima, will be demonstrating on Pearl Harbor Day.

December 1985

The War Against Capitalism

THE GREATEST intellectual achievement for man is to understand the relationship between capitalism and human dignity and the relationship between socialism and human abuse. Most of today's rhetoric about economic systems reverses reality. One of the best examples of this twisted thinking is found in the debate on South Africa.

Former Prime Minister Jan Smuts said, "It is ordained that we [Afrikaners], insignificant as we are, should be amongst the first people to begin the struggle against the new world tyranny of capitalism." Smuts' grievance, as with that of other architects of apartheid, is that the free market (capitalism) was no respecter of race, ethnicity, and religion.

They found that Afrikaner and English mine owners exhibited little ethnic solidarity in hiring decisions. They just hired the worker who could do the best work at the cheapest price. More often than not it was the South African black who got the job—and gained the skills. In 1924, the white Mine Workers Union said, "The real point on that is whites have been ousted by coloured labour." They complained that blacks were being hired instead of whites as common laborers for semi-skilled and skilled jobs. Union calls for government-backed discrimination were pleas for economic protection.

Leon Louw and Frances Kendall, in *South Africa: The Solution*, show that as early as 1870 black farmers were far more proficient than whites in agricultural output. To thwart the competition, the South African government erected an elaborate system of collusive laws and regulations to eliminate black farmers.

In many important ways South Africa's apartheid system is simply a struggle against the "injustices" of capitalism, namely its lack of respect for race. Socialism's government-control over the means of production *does* respect race, status, and other human characteristics. Law can make a mine owner hire a more expensive white when he would otherwise have hired a black. South Africa's apartheid system is riddled with white protection laws, ranging from job reservation to the Factory Acts. The thoroughness of South Africa's apartheid laws stand as testament to the parity of the free market.

Just ask yourself: Why are there racial laws in South Africa? When you see a law on the books, the most obvious reason is it's there because in its absence not everyone would behave according to the specifications of the law. Thus, the fact there are laws that say blacks cannot become engine drivers, elevator operators, and so forth, suggests that in the absence of these job reservation laws they would be hired for these jobs.

The true irony of the South African case is the people who want to help blacks are calling for socialism. But socialism is what blacks have had for years under the tight fist of the Afrikaners. What blacks need now is economic freedom: the right to work for whomever they please, the right to buy and sell whatever they want, and to trade with whomever they want.

South Africa isn't the only example of the brutality of socialism. In fact, the worst human abuses in modern history came under the auspices of socialism, namely, the National Socialist German Workers' Party. You and I know them as the Nazis. Look around the world, and whether your favorite socialist admits it or not, human abuse is associated with the government controls that accompany socialism and poverty. By contrast, people who enjoy the greatest degree of human rights tend also to enjoy less government and more wealth. If you think that's just a coincidence, think again!

June 1986

The Solution

SOUTH AFRICA has enacted stern "state of emergency" laws giving security forces broad powers of arrest and detention. It clamped down on news reporting from areas of unrest. What in the world are decent Americans to do about the state of affairs there?

The first order of business is to know more about the country's current state and its history. That can be found in a new book by Leon Louw, director of the Free Market Foundation of South Africa, and his wife, Frances Kendall, entitled, *South Africa: The Solution* (Amagi Publications, 1986).

The authors argue that in the early history of South Africa, blacks frequently outcompeted whites, especially in agriculture. The only way white farmers could compete with blacks was through a host of subsidies by South Africa's Agricultural Development Acts of 1904 and 1907. Levies and fees were imposed on black farmers with the result that they paid a higher percentage of their income in taxes than white farmers. The 1913 Land Act brought these pressures to their logical conclusion where blacks were reduced to mere farm wage-laborers.

The 1913 Land Act might be called the "father" of apartheid; it gave birth to hundreds of other laws and policies. Chief among these was Prime Minister Hertzog's "Civilized Labor" policy which is a system of protections to keep black workers from outcompeting white workers. The "civilized" labor policy had the support of white unionists, particularly Bill Andrews, labor leader and first secretary of South Africa's Communist Party. Andrews objected to what he called the "semi-slavery. . . of. . . dirty, evil-smelling Kaffirs [South Africa's derisive name for blacks]" because they were threatening the jobs of white miners by working for lower wages.

In 1924, the Socialist Labor and Afrikaner National Party Alliance (The Pact) unseated the South African Party. The banner they marched under read, "Workers of the World fight and unite for a white South Africa." After those elections, and well into the 1970s, the government worked at "perfecting" apartheid. Certain jobs were set aside for whites only (job reservation); areas were defined where blacks could live (Group Areas Act); cards were issued (pass laws); there was race certification (Population Registration Act); and in an effort to keep racial distinctions unblurred, laws preventing mixed marriages and interracial intercourse (Immorality Act). All these laws, and others, focused on the protection of whites from competition with blacks and included the economic tool of racists everywhere: *minimum wage laws.*

Despite continuing problems, South Africa *is* making significant changes in its apartheid system. Much of it is being done with the encouragement and assistance of the Free Market Foundation of South Africa. *The Solution* calls for the elimination of South Africa's brand of socialism and the formation of a free market. Louw and Kendall's political solution calls for setting up a weak central government and strong states along the lines of Switzerland's canton system. They call for full citizenship rights with a U.S.-type Bill of Rights, and the elimination of all racial laws.

Americans can speed the elimination of apartheid through our moral clout. Economic sanctions and other forms of punishment to bring South Africa to its economic knees are counterproductive. Ask yourself: Would American blacks have been helped had Jesse Owens not been allowed to compete in the Olympics? Or during the depression of the 1930s, could blacks have made the socioeconomic gains they made during the boom of the 1960s?

We need to condemn apartheid, not South Africa's blacks. Haven't they been hurt enough already?

July 1986

South Africa's Apartheid

IN EARLY July, I made my third visit to South Africa to deliver papers in conferences sponsored by the Witwatersrand University Department of Economics, the Free Market Foundation, and the Soweto Chamber of Commerce. My last visit was a ten week university lecture tour in 1980. From this most recent visit to Johannesburg, I can report South Africa is making significant progress in improving race relations despite misleading reports in our media and from advocates of economic sanctions.

Walking from my hotel to the downtown shopping area, I saw blacks working as sales clerks in department stores, supermarkets, and many other retail outlets. At major hotels such as the Carlton, Sunny Side, and Braamfontein, blacks were not only employed as receptionists, cashiers, and bellmen, they were also registered as guests and eating in the restaurants. All over Johannesburg blacks are visible as policemen and store security guards. In some major companies, particularly Western-owned firms, blacks are employed as managers and senior-level personnel. Job reservation laws, which kept certain jobs restricted, have all but disappeared. Remaining job reservation laws apply to mining where the Mineworkers Union maintains considerable political clout.

The fact of these and other changes may seem trivial to Americans who have forgotten our own not-too-distant past, but they were unthinkable in South Africa as recently as ten years ago. To put it in better perspective, Americans with a passport just go to the airport and they're off to England, France, or Japan. We consider that trivial. But what if you heard Russians and Eastern bloc citizens now had the same right? We'd applaud it as considerable progress.

The South African government is in the process of dismantling apartheid. The last remaining major apartheid law is the Group Areas Act which designates racial residences. The mayors of Durban and Capetown recently proposed their cities be used as initial experiments for its repeal. Under internal (and to some degree foreign) pressure, the South African government has recognized that the political franchise must be given to all citizens. They must now turn that recognition into reality.

Contrary to what's suggested in our media and by disinvestment advocates, the situation in South Africa is not one where whites are lined up against blacks. Many, if not most, whites want the government to eliminate apartheid. State President Botha's problem is to do it in a way so as not to lose his National Party constituency to white racist radicals like Terreblanche and Turnicht who have the charisma, cunning, and ruthlessness of Adolf Hitler. If these men come to power, they will have no reservations about using South Africa's awesome military might to slaughter thousands, even millions, of blacks in the name of law and order. They'd show no hesitancy to apply the same tools of the government against white "kaffir (nigger) lovers."

Contrary to what Americans are told, South African blacks do not speak with one voice on the direction and method of change. To expect otherwise would be absurd. To say the "*blacks* of South Africa" is just as foolish as saying the "whites of Europe"; it ignores important cultural differences. The French are different from the British, Germans from Swedes, Italians from Portuguese, and they don't love one another. Similarly, the Zulu differ from the Xhosa, the Sotho from the Venda, the Tswana from the Hottentot, and they don't necessarily love one another. Their major common interest is a hatred for apartheid; and like the European ethnics, with respect to Naziism in the 1930s and 1940s, they differ on the means to combat it.

July 1986

South Africa and the Media

SOUTH AFRICA'S apartheid system is as ugly as is oppression everywhere. But a consensus on this fact is no basis for the omissions and fabrications that have been served up by the media.

The world media would have us believe Bishop Desmond Tutu and the Reverend Alan Boseak speak for South African blacks. Neither man has a constituency in the sense of having been elected. On the other hand, Chief Mangosuthu Buthelezi is the minister of nearly 7 million Zulus of Kwazulu and elected head of Inkatha, South Africa's largest political organization. Yet he receives far less press coverage than either Tutu or Boseak.

Chief Buthelezi is of little interest to the press. He's portrayed as a government stooge, because he is against economic sanctions and violent confrontation with the government. Bthelezi says sanctions will aggravate the already bad economic condition of South African blacks. He asks whether blacks haven't suffered enough already at the hands of enemies? Why should they be punished at the hands of friends? In fact, complete sanctions would confer a one-time windfall gain for many white South Africans who could buy Western companies at depressed prices.

During my July visit to South Africa, I had a private meeting with

Chief Buthelezi, who is a personal friend. He told me that violent confrontation with the government is suicidal. The South African government has not used even 5 percent of its awesome power. Buthelezi is by no means a government stooge, as the press has painted him; he wisely believes conditions have not reached the point where violent confrontation and the loss of tens of thousands of lives is the only solution.

During our meeting, Buthelezi informed me of outright news manipulation. For example, black radicals would attack his people during a meeting or some other gathering. These attacks included fire bombings and assault, but what gets reported is his people retaliating. The media gives the impression that jailed African National Congress leader Nelson Mandela and Buthelezi are mortal enemies. But Buthelezi shared a handwritten letter from Mandela with me: "Your warm message of goodwill and support contributed tremendously to my speedy and complete recovery [from a prostate operation], and gave me much strength and joy. I shake your hands very warmly." Is this a communication between mortal enemies?

The American media tells us of "stayaways," strikes and boycotts, that are "this" percent and "that" percent effective, giving the impression of black unity. But what they withhold, for example, is that the current rent strike in Soweto is maintained through brutal coercion. Those Sowetans who want to pay their rent are prevented from doing so through intimidation and threats by the "comrades," who might be better described as young thugs. Blacks who want to work when a stayaway is called are threatened and harassed. Blacks who shop when a boycott has been called can be forced, by the comrades, to eat the soap they bought.

Being forced to eat soap is "mild" retribution. Crimes for which one can be punished by the comrades range from attending school, being a township official or policeman, or disobeying a stayaway. Punishment may be "necklacing," where a tire filled with gasoline is placed around your neck and set ablaze, or having your stomach slashed and filled with gasoline and ignited. Another variation is being forced to drink the gasoline which is then set ablaze. While all this is occurring, the comrades may dance around the victim, cutting and eating pieces of his flesh. Maids, servants, chauffeurs, and other workers told me the current state of emergency is tough, but it makes their lives safer. Chief

Buthelezi decries this black-on-black violence. One wonders whether the ANC and Western liberals would join in the condemnation.

These are just a few of the facts being kept from Americans. The tragedy is that Congress and the administration are moving ahead on policy without knowing the true state of affairs in South Africa. Such uninformed action may help in the fall elections, but it spells doom for millions of black and large and growing numbers of white South Africans who are hostile to the government's apartheid policy.

August 1986

I Think We Forgot

OUR JUDEO-CHRISTIAN values along with a generalized disposition toward liberty make us a great nation. We respect human dignity and prosperity, but by word and deed too many Americans assume freedom and prosperity are the rule and take them for granted. To the contrary, the history of man is one of not only poverty but brutal oppression and arbitrary control of the weak by powerful elites. For only a small part of man's history, and for only a tiny portion of the world's population, have we seen an exception to the history of brutality and material misery.

Our Judeo-Christian values and disposition toward liberty nurture dangers as well. They show up in our attitudes and perceptions of what is necessary to survive in a hostile world that, for the most part, is antagonistic toward liberty. Preachments of church leaders, diatribes by political spokesmen, and wild-eyed, wet-behind-the-ears college students calling for various forms of disarmament, show deathly naiveté of the real facts of life in this world.

Between World War I and World War II, the West virtually disarmed. We were lulled into complacency by Adolf Hitler who swore, "We have given guarantees for the states in the West. We have guaranteed to all contiguous neighbors the inviolability of their territory . . . . That is not a phrase—that is our sacred will. We are not interested in breaking peace." Shortly after these assurances were given, Hitler's tanks rolled into Czechoslovakia and Poland.

Those who warned of Germany's military designs faced Hitler's accusations of being "bloodthirsty warmongers." Hitler's most vicious verbal attacks were reserved for Winston Churchill, who did not see "peace in our time" as did Prime Minister Neville Chamberlain. Chamberlain thought Churchill's call for a defense buildup was unnecessary and might even provoke Hitler.

Forty years after a bloody World War II, we seem to have forgotten the costly lesson that treaties and promises are breakable. President Ronald Reagan, like Churchill earlier, has been urging us to militarily prepare ourselves and, like Churchill, he has been castigated as a warmonger. Just as in the 1930s, the propaganda is being orchestrated by a totalitarian beast—this time, it is Soviet General Secretary Mikhail Gorbachev.

Gorbachev is somewhat bolder than Hitler. He's singing peace and disarmament while U.S.S.R. troops engage in the brutal suppression of the Afghanistan people, while U.S.S.R. surrogates operate in Angola, Nicaragua, and Cambodia, and while at home, Russian Jews and dissidents face oppression and imprisonment.

Along with his Western sympathizers, Gorbachev not only calls for complete eradication of offensive nuclear weapons but of defensive nonnuclear systems as well. Even if the Russians could be trusted to honor a treaty banning nuclear weapons, it would be a bad treaty for us. The reason is simple. The West is outgunned and outmanned in conventional forces by Russia, China, and the Warsaw Pact nations. In a Warsaw Pact conventional attack on Europe, NATO forces could be expected to hold out for about a month before they would topple in utter defeat. The only thing that prevents attack is our nuclear umbrella. Gorbachev would love it if this nuclear deterrence was eliminated.

Hitler would have loved Gorbachev's propaganda advantage. With the growth of the welfare state in America, Gorbachev can offer our congressmen the irresistible temptation: Scrap the defense buildup, stop SDI, and in return you can spend more on pork barrel and social programs.

Military might is the only known deterrent to aggression. Totalitarians have no respect for treaties and promises.

November 1986

Suppressing the Moderates

C HIEF GATSHA Buthelezi has been visiting the United States and Canada over the last several weeks. Buthelezi is chief minister of the Zulus, South Africa's most numerous ethnic group, numbering some 7 million people, and elected leader of INKATHA, South Africa's largest black political organization. It will be my honor to introduce him at a Toronto luncheon sponsored by the Fraser Institute of Vancouver, British Columbia.

Buthelezi is part of the forces for sanity in South Africa. While the West worships the African National Congress' Oliver Tambo and Winnie Mandela, who call for violent confrontation and the murder of blacks they deem "sell-outs," Buthelezi seeks negotiation toward a peaceful settlement. Buthelezi is a lifelong foe of apartheid, but he's no fool; he understands that violent confrontation against South Africa's awesome military might is suicide.

This approach has won him the scorn of many, including the Congressional Black Caucus whose members refuse to meet with him. The Caucus also refused to meet with Bishop Abel Muzorewa of Zimbabwe in the 1970s and threw support to the Communist-backed Mugabe/ Nkomo forces. With the support of the U.S. and Andy Young, Robert Mugabe won and Zimbabweans have since lived under a state of emergency, like that in South Africa. Mugabe has had Joshua Nkomo under house arrest while government troops—largely of the Shona tribe—slaughter, rape, and plunder the Ndebele people. Yet there's not been one peep of protest from the Black Caucus, anti-apartheid groups, or liberals in Congress and around the nation.

The real tragedy of our sanctions policy toward South Africa is not that it's ineffective and hypocritical, but that it undermines both white and black forces for moderation. People like Buthelezi, Lucy Mvubelo, and many other black leaders are seen as ineffective. Moderate whites, such as Helen Suzman, Alan Paton, and P.W. Botha (South Africa's most progressive president) are viewed in the same light.

They're all against sanctions as are most black workers. Blacks from neighboring countries such as Zimbabwe, Zaire, Mozambique, Malawi and Lesotho, who legally and *illegally* enter South Africa, prefer the tangible benefits of food, housing, and jobs to the hypothetical benefits of a meaningless vote in their black states. They are voting with their feet for opportunities in South Africa that are threatened by sanctions.

When we imposed sanctions, important apartheid laws like job reservation, segregated theatres, stores, major hotels and restaurants, sports facilities, and universities, were either already—or in the process of being—repealed. Onerous pass laws had been relaxed. The Immorality and the Mixed Marriages acts were repealed. Just last month the powerful Afrikaner Dutch Reformed Church condemned apartheid.

Much more needs to be done; however, by not encouraging and rewarding these changes, we strengthen the hands of extremists—both black and white. In the face of these changes, President Botha is labeled a traitor by his political enemies like Turnicht and Terre Blanche. These men vociferously oppose his efforts to reduce apartheid. If these Hitlerites unseat Botha they'd have little reservation about slaughtering 4 to 5 million blacks in the name of preserving the white race.

The real hope for South Africa depends on whether people like Buthelezi can effect change before their Western "friends" help create conditions for a holocaust.

December 1986

Foreign Intrigue

THERE ARE plenty of problems in U.S. foreign policy. The Reagan-Iran-Nicaragua arms snafu is just a symptom. But before we get down to *the* problem, let's focus a bit on some of the political debris that's surfaced in the revelation of our multi-million-dollar arms shipment to Iran.

We should not negotiate with terrorists or their mediators. No single American's life is worth risking the welfare and security of the entire nation. The Reagan administration was dead wrong to ship arms to Iran in a bid to spring hostages.

Its contention that the arms shipment was not tribute but an attempt to influence those in Iran considered more friendly to the U.S. carries a bit more merit, but not much. What congressman would have condemned President Franklin Roosevelt on the finding he was responsible for the shipment of arms to anti-Hitler factions in Germany? The Ayatollah Khomeini and Adolf Hitler are kissing cousins. If the fly-by-night intrigue of the arms deal was meant to undermine the Ayatollah, it might make a wee bit of sense. Still, one wonders how anybody in the White House could have been naive enough to think the deal could have been kept secret.

And what about the Nicaragua connection? The *contras* need more money to fight the Russian- and Cuban-backed Sandinista forces, and Congress has belatedly allotted only $100 million. We must do something about Russia seeking a stronghold in Latin America. In that sense, one can sympathize with the administration for seeking ways to increase *contra* aid in the face of our appeasement-oriented Congress. These congressmen see our action as interference in the domestic affairs of a sovereign nation and prefer to wait for Soviet missiles to be in place before they act.

The Reagan-Iran-Nicaragua connection appears to be unnecessary intrigue by the world's richest, most powerful nation. Let me lay out the bare bones of what I believe should be our foreign policy.

The fact that we are the most ingenious people on earth and have an economic system capable of letting that ingenuity climb to heights heretofore unknown to man means we do not have to resort to intrigue. Instead, and far simpler, we can just out-produce our enemies. In other words, we can produce more, and superior, weapons and defense systems than any assortment of our present adversaries—Russia, China, and the Warsaw Pact nations—and with less sacrifice of our national resources to boot. We don't have to play cloak-and-dagger games; we can mind our business until our interests are threatened.

We have a history of failing to use our strength. When we had the monopoly on nuclear weapons, we should have handed out an ultimatum to the rest of the world: "If you build nuclear weapon facilities, we're going to bomb them." When the Russians built the Berlin Wall, we should have leveled it with our bulldozers. The Bay of Pigs invasion shouldn't have been conducted by a bunch of poorly trained Cuban exiles but by several U.S. Marine brigades. Now, instead of horsing around with the *contras,* we should call out the Marines and gunboats.

Setting a sound foreign policy is a challenge requiring sacrifice. Meeting this challenge is a must, if our freedom and the little bit that exists elsewhere is to survive and grow.

December 1986